THE ONE TRUTH

CONTEXTUAL ABSOLUTISM AND THE BATTLE FOR DOCTRINAL CLARITY

L. J. ANDERSON

LAMAD PRESS

CONTENTS

Dedication   1

Abstract   2

Preface   4

Why Truth Matters More Than Ever   8

1. What Is Truth?   12

2. There Is Only One Truth Per Question   22

3. Truth and God: Singular Truth in Scripture   30

4. Truth vs. Perspective: A Look at Contextual   43
    Truths

5. Why Christians Disagree   56

6. How to Discover the Truth (Without Falling   74
    into Error)

7. Why Truth Demands Action   93

8. Formalizing Contextual Absolutism   102

A Brief Call to Action   111

Also by L. J. Anderson   112

Bibliography   114

A Note to Scholars and Critics   118

About the author   120

To Quinn and Malachi,
may you grow in your love for the truth
and the one from whom all truth originates

ABSTRACT

The One Truth: Contextual Absolutism and the Battle for Doctrinal Clarity presents a bold claim: every question in life and theology has exactly one correct answer, even if that truth is complex and difficult to articulate. In an age where relativism dominates cultural discourse and doctrinal disagreement is treated as inevitable, or even desirable, this book challenges both the church, and by extension, the world to return to a biblical and philosophical understanding of truth as singular, objective, and discoverable.

Author L. J. Anderson dismantles the modern myth that conflicting perspectives can all be valid, showing through accessible examples (like the 6-or-9 illusion, the half-empty glass, and even pineapple pizza) that disagreement is often a matter of faulty perception, not competing truths. Drawing from Scripture, logic, and theological reflection, Anderson explains why truth must govern not only our moral and spiritual convictions but our doctrinal formulations as well.

Designed for lay readers, pastors, students, and thoughtful Christians, this book lays the philosophical groundwork for Anderson's broader theological vision, including his development of Structural Theism. It equips readers to reject relativism, think clearly, and pursue truth with conviction, regardless of tradition, popularity, or pressure to compromise.

PREFACE

The book you are reading is unapologetically independently published.[1] Independent publishing offers many benefits and only a few significant drawbacks, namely, the lack of peer review and brand recognition. Authors who are not yet widely known often depend on the credibility of the publisher's name. Peer review, for its part, plays an important role in academic publishing, acting as a gatekeeper to prevent poor scholarship from reaching publication. Where possible, I welcome peer-reviewed engagement with these ideas in journal articles, responses, and academic dialogue.

However, peer review does not guarantee high-quality work, just as the absence of peer review does not necessarily imply poor quality. In many ways, true peer review begins after publication, when the broader academic community has the opportunity to evaluate and respond to the work. In

---

1. It should be noted that Lamad Press is not a vanity or pay-to-publish service. It is the author's personal scholarly imprint, established to house a single, coherent body of theological research. The purpose is to develop this work with academic rigor and present it transparently for open review, allowing the arguments to stand or fall on their own merit.

this model, peer engagement happens post-publication, as scholars interact with the material in print, online forums, public reviews, and future publications.

While still largely untested, this publishing model shows promise as an alternative method of making academic research accessible. The majority of scholars continue to view independent publishing as significantly inferior to peer-reviewed articles or works released by traditional academic presses.

The following note expands on the mission behind Lamad Press and my broader goals as an independent scholar-publisher.

Theological Publishing with Purpose

L. J. Anderson is pioneering a new approach to theological scholarship, one that is academically rigorous, biblically faithful, and institutionally independent.

Through Lamad Press, he is constructing a publishing model that restores Scripture as the primary authority in theological method while engaging seriously with the philosophical and historical challenges of Christian doctrine. His work seeks not merely to critique existing systems but to build constructive theological models that speak to the most enduring tensions in Christian thought.

At the heart of this mission is Anderson's development of Structural Theism, a theological framework that accounts for the internal identity of God by emphasizing divine structure over classical simplicity. Structural Theism affirms the reality of Trinitarian distinction, upholds the relational depth of God revealed in Scripture, and seeks to avoid the conceptual pitfalls of both eternal generation and impersonal metaphysics. It is a model designed to preserve God's oneness and threeness without collapsing into modalism, metaphysical abstraction, or tritheism.

One key expression of this model is the Incarnational Monogenetic Model, which offers a biblically grounded alternative to the doctrine of eternal generation by locating the Son's identity not in timeless derivation, but in his incarnational role and mission as uniquely begotten of the Father.

Unlike traditional academic pathways bound by institutional gatekeeping and publishing delays, Anderson's independent model allows for timely, coherent, and accessible scholarship, published through Lamad Press and distributed by Lamad Christian Books. His aim is to demonstrate that it is possible to do theology that is both deeply scholarly and uncompromisingly biblical, outside the confines of conventional academic systems.

Rooted in Tradition

Independent theological publishing is not a modern innovation; rather, it is a return to Christian tradition. From the Church Fathers to the Reformers, many of the most influential theologians operated outside formal institutions, writing and distributing works grounded in theological conviction, fidelity to Scripture, and service to the church. Lamad Press stands in that same stream, reviving a historic model for a new generation of biblical theology.

WHY TRUTH MATTERS MORE THAN EVER

Despite what many seem to think, theology is not a buffet that we can pick and choose from. I cannot choose a particular flavor of a given doctrine just because there is historical precedent for it. Truth demands something much more robust than that. In contemporary theology, the major concern is unity. Biblically, the church is commanded to be one but, clearly, this is not the case today. The church is fundamentally divided and continues to divide more every day. To combat this, many churches and theologians hold to some form of ecumenism, at least in idea, if not in actuality. Ecumenism is based on the idea that we can agree to disagree so long as we all uphold a certain set of doctrines which are typically said to be "essential" to the faith and that doing so defends Christian unity. However, the claim that Christians shouldn't argue about "nonessentials" may sound peaceable, but it quietly implies that some revealed truths of Scripture are functionally optional. More extreme versions of this fall into functional religious pluralism, which is the view that there are many paths to God. The problem with all of this is that Scripture does not uphold this view, nor does it mean that we should not have grace with one another as we seek truth. That said, grace is not a license to accept contradiction. It is the posture we adopt as we pursue clarity together. A robust defense of the last few statements is the subject of another book. This book, however, provides the logical and biblical basis for understanding what truth is and how we are to go about seeking it. Broadly speaking, *The One Truth* defends the concept that truth is singular both biblically and logically. It is meant to provide an epistemological foundation for seeking truth as Christians.

The One Truth is designed to make you think about truth claims. To illustrate the kind of thing I hope you will be able to analyze after this book is finished, let me present to you a quote from *Star Wars* (spoilers ahead). In Episode 3, Anakin Skywalker, a troubled young Jedi Knight (think space wizard), turns to the dark side of the force (think of "Chi" and similar concepts from Eastern religions) and becomes a Sith Lord (a *bad* space wizard) known as Darth Vader. He is confronted by Obi-Wan Kenobi, his former master who remains a Jedi Master. Prior to a big, epic fight scene, Obi-Wan tries to reason with Anakin. Eventually, Anakin makes the following statement: "If you're not with me, then you're my enemy!" Obi-Wan responded, "Only a Sith deals in absolutes. I will do what I must."

Did you catch it? Obi-Wan made a truth claim about the Sith... and by doing so declared himself a Sith. He said, "*Only* a Sith deals in absolutes," which is, itself, an absolute statement. Thus, if *only Sith* deal in absolutes, then Obi-Wan is a Sith. Obi-Wan made a truth claim that is self-refuting. Unfortunately, many in the world today do the exact same thing. Someone saying to me, "My truth is my truth, and your truth is your truth" is functionally no different. What they are saying, in function, is this: "Every person has their own truth." But that is a *universal* truth claim. *They* are telling *me* that their truth is truth and my truth is truth, but what if I disagree? Aren't they telling me what my truth is? They have decided they are the arbiter of truth over everyone else while trying to claim that there is no universal truth.

Christians will rarely say things like that, at least on the surface. That said, when we hear phrases like "we must agree to disagree" that is a subtle infiltration of relativism into the church, particularly when it is intended to shut down dialogue. It implies that we can both reasonably hold our positions. The problem is that this is not how truth works. Unfortunately, few truly seek the truth. We have grown complacent with what we believe rather than seeking for the truth.

Why This Book?

This book has a two-fold purpose. On the one hand, it is an apologetic defense of truth over and against both moral and religious relativism, as I have been laying out in this introduction. It is designed to teach you how to evaluate truth claims and be able to discover the truth for yourself. This is a huge deal in our culture today. Additionally, this book would make an excellent addition to a course on epistemology, apologetics, or hermeneutics. But that is not my entire reason for writing this book. The other hand that needs to be shown is that I am writing this book to defend my methodology. I write books that are polemic. They unapologetically seek to demolish bad reasoning and exegesis and build something that can take its place based on Scripture and sound reason. As such, *The One Truth* is an apologetic for my method. It answers several questions. Why do I write the books I write? Why am I so unwilling to compromise? From the reader's angle, it answers questions like, "How does L. J. Anderson get to the positions he gets to?"

Also, if you are looking for a more "formal" introduction to the logic behind *The One Truth*, Chapter 8 lays the foundation for Contextual Absolutism using formal logic, a formal definition, and engages with the core axioms.

CHAPTER ONE

WHAT IS TRUTH?

THE QUESTION OF TRUTH is quite philosophical in nature, but it is imperative to answer it in our quest to defend the faith from attacks originating both outside the church and from within. Essentially any class on apologetics will include some philosophy because it is typically the world's philosophies that we are defending Christianity against. Thus, answering the age-old question "What is truth?" is at the base of many discussions surrounding Scripture. However, it is of particular importance today as the general assertion is that truth is relative. A typical Christian philosopher's definition of "truth" is "that which accords with reality" or something very similar.[1] This is an accurate definition, but it does not do a good job of demonstrating what this looks like exactly. This defini-

---

1. Consider, for example, chapter two of Paul M. Gould, Travis Dickinson, and R. Keith Loftin's *Stand Firm: Apologetics and the Brilliance of the Gospel* (Nashville, TN: B&H Academic, 2018).

tion is a type of correspondence view of truth.[2] Meaning, that truth *corresponds* to what is really real. This is not the prevailing view of the world right now. The prevailing worldview (some form of relativism) is often diametrically opposed to what the Bible says. The Bible is chock-full of truth claims and the world's response is often nearly the opposite of what Scripture says, for example:

- The Bible says that God created everything in six days according to his design. The world says the universe came into being by random chance and that everything as we know it came through a process of minute changes over billions of years.[3]

- The Bible says that man is sinful and deserves death. The world says humans are basically good. For example, humanistic psychology assumes, "Humans are innately good, which means there is nothing inherently negative or evil about them (humans)."[4]

---

2. Norman Geisler, *The Big Book of Christian Apologetics: An A to Z Guide* (Grand Rapids, MI: Baker Books, 2012), 884-85. Geisler shows that this view of truth can be traced to Plato. He was the main one who systematically engaged with the idea that truth corresponds to reality.

3. Robert Jastrow, *God and the Astronomers* (New York: W. W. Norton & Company, 1992), 8.

4. Saul Mcleod, "Humanistic Approach in Psychology (Humanism): Definition & Examples," *Simply Psychology*. December 20, 2023. https://www.simplypsychology.org/humanistic.html.

- The Bible says that there is "man" and "woman." The world says we can choose our own gender, and that gender is a social construct.[5]

- The Bible says that there is one God. The world says either that there is no God or that all gods are equally valid, and we cannot place one above another.[6]

As we can quickly see, the truth claims of the Bible are often flipped on their head by the world, particularly in the current relativistic culture.

Nevertheless, the answer to the question "What is truth?" is the same regardless of the topic. So, having a firm grasp of the concept of truth will be beneficial across the board. In addition to giving you a good idea of what truth is, I am going to make a massive claim and, by the end of this book, I hope to have proven said claim to you. Here's the claim: *Every topic has one ultimate truth, though our statements about it may vary in length, depth, or precision.* I am not going to explain this claim in this chapter, as that is the subject of Chapter 2. However, before moving to defend this claim, we need to look at how many things *appear* relativistic but are not in actuality. Truth does not

---

5. Lisa M. Diamond and Molly Butterworth, "Questioning Gender and Sexual Identity: Dynamic Links over Time," *Sex Roles*, 59 (5–6): 365–376. doi:10.1007/s11199-008-9425-3.

6. Joseph Runzo, "God, Commitment, and Other Faiths: Pluralism vs. Relativism," *Faith and Philosophy*, 5 (1988): 353–57.

bend based on our viewpoint, despite what relativists want to claim. My truth is true *if and only if* said truth aligns with reality.

Most people have seen a picture like this:

This is a pretty common example of how perspective seems to change the truth. In fact, this is exactly what the cartoonist is typically trying to get at. I say "typically" be-cause, in this case, I made this cartoon, and it was not my intent to demonstrate relativity. The argument is that the number is different depending on how you look at it. But that is not how numbers work. Numbers, in every instance *except* in pictures like this, always have *one* meaning. In other words, this is *either* a "6" or a "9". It cannot be both. We determine this primarily through context. For example, if there is other writing or numbers nearby, we can ascertain the correct number by comparing it to what is around it. However, even if there is no context to tell us what number it is, it *still* is either a "6" or a "9". The only way to know for sure what the number is supposed to be in a case like this is to ask the person who wrote it. In summary, *one* of the guys above is correct and the other is wrong.

Another example is a half-full/half-empty glass of wa-ter. See this glass?

Would you say this glass is half full or half empty? Though this question is often used to determine if you are an optimist or a pessimist, there is actually a correct answer to this question. If you have seen *Finding Nemo* you will likely remember the scene where Marlin and Dory are in a whale's mouth. In this scene, Marlin makes a statement about how the whale's mouth is already half empty. Dory countered by saying, "Hmm, I'd say it's half full." Marlin shot back with something like, "The water's going *down*. It's half empty!" This appears to be a fun quip about the difference between an optimist and a pessimist. However, Marlin is *completely correct* in his assessment. If the last thing that happened to a cup of water is that it was filled halfway, then it is half full. If the water was poured out or drunk until it was emptied halfway, then it is half empty. When I did this illustration for a class, I filled the glass up and then left it alone. In this case, this glass was half full. I filled it up halfway and didn't touch it afterward. If I had filled it up all the way and then drunk half of it, it would have been half empty. We will come back to this example in a later chapter.

The final example I want to discuss is gravity. Gravity appears to be relative does it not? After all, on earth, we experience more gravity than we would on the moon and less than we would if we could stand on the surface of the sun. But, as you have probably guessed by now, gravity is not relative, at least not in the way it seems. You see, there is what is called a gravitational constant. This constant is, well, *constant*. It does not change anywhere in this universe. The *force* of gravity exerted between two objects changes based on certain factors—namely, the mass of each object and the distance between the centers of the two masses. If you know those things and the gravitational constant, then you can calculate the force of gravity anywhere in the universe. This equation is itself a truth statement about the force of gravity in the universe and looks like this when in a mathematical formula:

$$F_g = \frac{Gm_1 m_2}{r^2}$$

This concept continues in every case where there seem to be multiple truth statements. There is only one statement that is fully true even though there may appear to be multiple true statements.

What I find interesting is that this questioning of truth is not a modern invention, though it has been exacerbated in modern times by relativism. So far, we have looked specifically at physical truths. That said, the same principles above apply perfectly to God and his Word. For example, in John 18:37, Jesus made a defense before Pontius Pilate saying, "You say that I am a king. For this purpose I was born and for this purpose I have come into this world—to bear witness to the truth. Everyone who is of the truth listens to my voice." To this, Pilate replied, "What is truth?" and promptly walked away from *the* authority on truth, the Creator of the universe. Jesus made the claim, "I am *the* way, *the* truth, and *the* life." In fact, God and his salvation story operate on this kind of exclusivity. There isn't a myriad of ways to God, only one: belief in Jesus. There aren't hundreds or thousands of gods, there is only one. Jesus isn't *a* god; he is *the* God and the second Person of the Trinity. The list goes on and on.

Summary

This chapter addresses the philosophical and theological importance of defining truth in a culture dominated by relativism. While Christian philosophers often define truth as "that which accords with reality" (a correspondence view), this definition must be illustrated in practice. Using examples like the "6 or 9" illustration, the half-full/half-empty glass, and the gravitational constant, the author shows that apparent relativity usually masks an objective, singular truth that can be discovered through context or authoritative clarification. Truth does not bend to personal perspective and there is always one ultimate truth for any topic, though our descriptions may vary in depth or precision. This applies not only to physical realities but also to theological ones: Scripture's truth claims are absolute, Christ himself is truth, and salvation is found exclusively in him. Pilate's dismissal of truth when face-to-face with Jesus serves as a warning against ignoring the only true source of reality.

Discussion Questions:

Summarize this chapter in your own words.

How does the correspondence view of truth ("that which accords with reality") challenge the modern assumption that truth is subjective or personal?

In what ways do the "6 or 9" and "half-full/half-empty" illustrations expose flaws in relativistic thinking? Can you think of additional everyday examples where truth appears relative but is not?

How do cultural beliefs about creation, human nature, gender, and religion directly contradict the Bible's claims? Why is it important for Christians to recognize and address these contradictions?

How might the concept of one ultimate truth per topic change the way we approach theological disagreements within the church?

Why is it significant that Jesus not only claimed to speak the truth but to *be* the truth (John 14:6)? How does this shape our understanding of all other truth claims?

Pilate's question, "What is truth?" was followed by walking away from Jesus. What might this reveal about our culture's tendency to dismiss or avoid ultimate truth, and how should Christians respond?

Chapter Two

There Is Only One Truth Per Question

Last chapter, I made a very bold claim. I wrote: *Every topic has one ultimate truth, though our statements about it may vary in length, depth, or precision.* This claim is rather provocative and I began to tease out some of what that might mean with the illustrations provided in the last chapter. However, now I need to defend this statement.

I do not mean to say that a single sentence can accurately state the truth in every case. A truth statement can range anywhere from a paragraph to twenty pages long or longer in order to give an accurate statement about whatever topic or question is being discussed. It is even possible that a given truth statement would need 1000 pages to fully develop. Much like a statement to the police can be short or exceedingly long depending on the situation, so too can a truth statement be short or long depending on the object or idea in question. It is also possible to have different *types* of truth statements for a given object. For example, you might see a dog and rightly call it a dog. This is a completely true statement in and of itself; however, it is also a very generic and imprecise truth statement. If you needed to tell someone who didn't see the dog about the dog, you would need to be much more precise about the truth statement. You might need to say that it was a German Shepherd or a large black dog. In more extreme cases, you might need to provide a precise, scientific definition about the dog. Thus, a truth statement can change depending on what the context demands, but this is a question of *precision* rather than different truths.

While the need, or lack thereof, of being precise in a truth statement is something that happens on a daily basis, the attempt to shorten a truth claim when it needs to be longer is a dangerous endeavor that will likely result in a false or somewhat inaccurate truth statement. For example, you have likely heard the phrase "Love God, love others." Jesus' teaching on the greatest commandment is commonly summarized this way. What makes it dangerous to narrow what Jesus said down to this? It loses the *how*, the *who*, and the *weight* of the Old Testament. In other words, it loses its *context*. You see, Jesus was quoting the Old Testament when he said, "Love the Lord your God with all your heart and with all your soul and with all your mind and with all your strength," and "love your neighbor as yourself" (Matthew 22:37–39). Not only that though, but the situation he was in was meant to be impossible. The guy, who asked him to state the greatest commandment in the Law was essentially a lawyer of the Old Testament. He knew the Old Testament inside and out and was trying to *trap* Jesus. He

anticipated Jesus saying something like "You shall not murder," which, though important, is not the greatest commandment. Rather than giving a single commandment as
anticipated, Jesus answered by summing up the *entire* Law
and Prophets with the two commandments he gave.[1] By
shortening what Jesus said to "Love God, love others," we
lose the whole weight of the Old Testament. Additionally,
we don't know *how* we are to love God and others, nor do
we know *who* we are to love. Which God are we to love?
Yahweh? Zeus? Ba'al? Jesus' statement tells us these things;
"Love God, love others" does not. In fact, "Love God, love
others" is a true statement to the question of "What is the
greatest commandment" *if and only if* the one saying it and
the one hearing it have the right contextual background
to understand what this means exactly. To say this to anyone without the proper background information to understand what it means, is to simply invite error. If I say "Love
God, love others" to a Muslim, they would immediately
think of something that I did not mean. The same is true
even for Christians. Unless one knows which God I am
talking about, what "love" means (a huge question in our
current culture), and how we are to display it toward both
God and others, I am likely doing a form of false teaching.
It would not be *intentional* false teaching, and it may not
qualify as technical false teaching either. But practically
speaking, it is miscommunication that opens the door to

---

1. R. T. France, *Matthew: An Introduction and* Commentary (Downers
Grove, IL: InterVarsity Press, 1985), 323.

false interpretation, and that alone makes it dangerous. The impact of what I would be saying is not what I would be going for and the result would almost certainly be letting my listeners construct their own definition of what it means to love God and others. In summary, oversimplification, in many cases, can and does result in distorted or easily misunderstood truth statements. It is often much better to take the time to develop a more accurate, albeit longer, truth statement, especially for very important objects (such as God and how we are to relate to him).

In the end, we must recognize that a single object or idea can have multiple truth statements depending on the level of abstraction and the semantic content required by the context. Saying, "That is a dog" is true but so is saying "That is a large black German Shepherd trained for law enforcement." These are not competing truths but different expressions of the same reality, suited to different needs. Theological statements work the same way. Saying "Jesus is Lord" is entirely true, but it may need pages of explanation depending on who's listening. The truth remains the same, but our clarity depends on communicating the full semantic content required for understanding. Oversimplification, especially when dealing with God, is not faithfulness. It is often carelessness. Truth may be singular, but if we fail to express it clearly at the level the situation demands, we risk distorting it. Therefore, our task is not merely to affirm the truth, but to speak it well.

Still, we must ask: if truth is singular, why do Christians disagree? The answer is not that truth is flexible, but that humans are fallible. To be fallible is to be capable of failing. Everyone, except God, is capable of failing and we do so regularly; however, there is hope for failing *less*. When two Christians disagree on a theological issue, at least one of them is wrong, possibly both. The problem is never with the truth itself but with our approach to it. In chapter five, I will explore why these disagreements happen, examining how misplaced authorities, selective interpretations, and even a lack of sufficient biblical data can all contribute to Christians arriving at different conclusions. But let me be clear: disagreement is not something to celebrate. It is something to grieve, to investigate, and, whenever possible, to resolve through greater submission to God's Word.

Summary

This chapter defends the assertion that all topics have one ultimate truth, even though the expression of that truth may vary in length, complexity, or specificity. Drawing from analogies (e.g., describing a dog) and biblical examples (e.g., Jesus' answer regarding the greatest commandment), the chapter argues that differences in precision and contextual clarity do not indicate multiple truths, but rather varied articulations of the same truth. Theological truth, particularly statements about God, doctrine, and Scripture, requires careful attention to context, audience, and semantic fullness. The common phrase "Love God, love others" is examined as a potentially dangerous oversimplification that can mislead if divorced from its biblical roots and contextual richness. The chapter concludes by anticipating the objection of doctrinal disagreement among Christians, asserting that such disagreements stem not from truth's ambiguity but from human fallibility. Faithfulness to truth demands not merely affirming true propositions but expressing them with the depth and clarity appropriate to the situation.

Discussion Questions:

Summarize this chapter in your own words.

What do people typically mean when they say, "There are multiple truths"?

Why is it dangerous to oversimplify biblical statements?

How might this chapter change how you approach theological debates?

Do you agree that disagreement among Christians is something to be grieved? Why or why not?

How can pastors and teachers balance brevity with doctrinal precision in preaching and discipleship?

In what ways can theological slogans (e.g., "God is love") be both helpful and harmful? Provide other examples.

CHAPTER THREE

TRUTH AND GOD: SINGULAR TRUTH IN SCRIPTURE

U P UNTIL THIS POINT, we have primarily looked at philosophy, asking the broad questions of what "truth" is and how truth and perspective work together. Now, it is time to turn to Scripture and God. How does truth show itself as singular in Scripture? This chapter is going to be commentary-like. It pulls a bunch of uniqueness claims together and briefly engages with them to demonstrate that Christianity is built on exclusivity. Either it is true, or it isn't.

Jesus' Claim to Be "*The* Truth"

The exclusivity of Christ is woven into the very fabric of biblical revelation. Scripture does not allow us to entertain a relativistic view of truth, salvation, or God. It is not just Jesus who makes exclusive claims about himself. The entire Bible proclaims a vision of reality in which there is only one God, only one way to be reconciled to him, and only one truth to be believed.

Jesus' claim in John 14:6 is as bold as it is exclusive: "I am the way, and the truth, and the life. No one comes to the Father except through me." Here, Jesus is not suggesting that he is one path among many, but that he is the only path to God. This declaration doesn't just set Jesus apart. It defines him as the singular revelation of God's truth and the sole avenue of reconciliation between God and man. Jesus' role as the truth and the life is not metaphorical or poetic. It is a direct statement of exclusivity. He does not point to truth as one of many enlightened teachers; he is the truth. Any attempt to reduce him to just another wise teacher or religious leader undermines his own testimony and the entire biblical witness.

Acts 4:12 reinforces this: "There is salvation in no one else, for there is no other name under heaven given to people by which we must be saved." Peter is issuing a categorical truth claim. No religious figure, no philosophical system, no cultural moralism, nothing outside of Jesus can save. If that sounds harsh, it's only because we've been conditioned to think truth should be soft and inclusive. But truth, by definition, excludes what is false.

The Shema declares, "Hear Israel, Yahweh our God, Yahweh is one" (Deuteronomy 6:4, my translation),[1] emphasizing the uniqueness and unity of the one true God.

---

1. It can also be rendered, "Hear, O Israel, Yahweh is our God, Yahweh is one." This makes more sense in English, but is not necessarily what is being said in Hebrew.

Paul affirms this in 1 Timothy 1:17 by praising "the only God". That same God sent his "only begotten Son" (John 3:16, my translation), who openly declared, "I and the Father are one" (John 10:30). Taken together, these passages form a coherent theological foundation: there is one God, and Jesus is his only Son who is truly divine and sent to redeem mankind in a way no other figure in any religion can.

Isaiah 45 contains an unflinching barrage of exclusive claims from Yahweh himself: "I am Yahweh, and there is no other, besides me there is no God" (verse 5), and again, "There is no god besides me, a righteous God and a Savior; there is none besides me" (verse 21).[2] Yahweh is not one god among others. He is the only God who exists, and he alone can save.

Paul makes this even clearer in 1 Corinthians 8:4–6.

---

2. All Old Testament references to the divine name are written as "Yahweh". Unless I provide my own translation, the verses quoted in this book are from the ESV, but I am unwilling to obscure God's name to appease a tradition of men—even a tradition that began with good intentions. The most used word in the entire Bible, if one discounts pronouns and similar words, is "Yahweh". In fact, it is used nearly 7,000 times which indicates its importance. We would do well to remember to give God's name its proper weight. To not do so, is to take the name of Yahweh in vain (Exodus 20:7). This verse essentially means that we are not to make the name of Yahweh worthless. In an attempt to avoid the judgment of the third of the ten commandments, the Jews refused to speak the name of Yahweh. By doing so they made his name *worthless* because they forgot what it was. I will not make the same mistake. This is a personal conviction that I believe has significant merit. God gives great weight to his name, and I cannot go against him by lessening it.

Though acknowledging that "indeed there are many 'gods' and many 'lords'"—in other words, that people believe in all sorts of divine figures—he immediately draws the line: "Yet for us there is one God, the Father... and one Lord, Jesus Christ." The Christian confession excludes the validity of all contrary claims. Any worldview or religious system that contradicts the one true God is false.

Even the First Commandment demonstrates this: "You shall have no other gods before me" (Exodus 20:3). While some might quibble by saying that this demonstrates that there *are* other gods, Scripture is clear that even though there are "gods" they are not real. Exodus 20:3 is a demand for total allegiance. To obey it is more than just avoiding pagan idols. It also includes rejecting every ideology, philosophy, or modern compromise that dares to put something else in the place only Yahweh deserves. And yes, that includes the idol of relativism.

Exclusive truth claims offend the spirit of our age. But the Bible simply declares the truth and holds every person accountable for how they respond. The claim that Jesus is the only way is a wide invitation through the *only* door that leads to life.

And if you're wondering how Jesus can declare that he *is* the truth, especially given the model I lay out in this book, which says every topic or question has exactly one truth claim, then hold that question. In the next chapter, we're going to look at something called contextual truths, which is the base of Contextual Absolutism. To be understood rightly, all truth must have context. While all truth must be understood in the right context, some truth needs a specific type of context (a condition) to go into effect. These are truths that operate on conditions—meaning they are true, *if and only if* a certain context is in place. This will help us explain how Jesus is the truth in a way that preserves both the exclusivity of his identity and the internal logic of truth itself. But for now, this much is apparent: Jesus taught and embodied truth in the most unapologetic way imaginable. And he did so in a world that has always preferred lies.

Scripture's Other Exclusive Claims

The exclusivity of Scripture is not limited to salvation and the identity of God. It extends to every doctrine it teaches. Christianity does not offer a buffet of spiritual ideas to pick and choose from. It offers coherent, exclusive, and, in most cases, clear truth. When Scripture speaks on a topic, it speaks with authority, not suggestion. We are not free to reinterpret or relativize doctrines simply because they touch cultural nerves or personal preferences. The Word of God gives singular answers. We are expected to conform.

Take marriage, for example. In Matthew 19:4–6, Jesus appeals to the created order, not to cultural custom. "Have you not read," he says, "that he who created them from the beginning made them male and female, and said, 'Therefore a man shall leave his father and his mother and hold fast to his wife, and the two shall become one flesh'?" He concludes, "What therefore God has joined together, let not man separate." His statement went against the prevailing idea that a man can divorce his wife for any reason. Marriage, according to Jesus, is between one man and one woman, bound together by God himself and that breaking the marriage is breaking what God himself put together.

Divorce is not left to opinion or circumstance. In the very same chapter, Jesus states that anyone who divorces his spouse, except for sexual immorality, and marries another commits adultery (Matthew 19:9). The Pharisees wanted to debate degrees of permissibility. Jesus silenced the argument by appealing to God's original design and insisting that the truth had already been spoken. The Word doesn't flex with culture. It calls culture to repentance.

Consider gender and identity. Deuteronomy 22:5 declares, "A woman shall not wear a man's garment, nor shall a man put on a woman's cloak, for whoever does these things is an abomination to the Lord your God." The point here is not fashion. It's about the sacred distinction between male and female. The categories are not fluid. They are fixed. This is not an isolated verse. The entire creation narrative hinges on this binary reality (Genesis 1:27), and every doctrine that follows—including leadership, family structure, and spiritual roles—flows from that foundation.

All three doctrines listed above in this section are what many would consider peripheral, or secondary, doctrines. They are not salvific doctrines, which are typically the only ones considered "essential" to the faith.[3] That said, Scripture still makes exclusive claims regarding them. Jude 3 urges believers to "contend for the faith that was once for all delivered to the saints." That phrase "once for all" is crucial. Doctrinal truth has been revealed. It is not evolving with the times or expanding to include new ideas. It is fixed. Settled. Exclusive. The *applications* of this settled doctrinal truth are varied and depend on context; however, the truth itself is set, even if we don't know it perfectly.

Titus 1:9 commands church leaders to "hold firm to the trustworthy word as taught," not creatively reinterpret it. Hebrews 13:9 warns against being "led away by diverse and strange teachings". Why? Because there is one true doctrine. Anything else is, by definition, false. The goal of theology is to discern the one position that aligns with God's Word in full, not to make God's Word teach what we want it to teach.

If Scripture Is True, It Speaks with One Voice

If Scripture is true (meaning it is inerrant and infallible), then it does not merely *contain* truth.[4] It *is* truth. And if it is truth, it cannot contradict itself. But this principle goes

---

3. David S. Dockery and Christopher W. Morgan, eds, *Christian Higher Education: Faith, Teaching, and Learning in the Evangelical Tradition* (Wheaton, IL: Crossway, 2018), 23.

4. Gregg R. Allison, *The Baker Compact Dictionary of Theological Terms* (Grand Rapids, MI: Baker Books, 2016), 79.

even deeper. Scripture doesn't just avoid contradiction. It speaks with one voice because it has one Author. Though penned by dozens of human writers over the course of fifteen hundred years, the Word of God is ultimately authored by God himself. It is a unified revelation.

This is one of the most overlooked doctrines in modern theology. Too many treat Scripture as a dialogue between perspectives. Paul versus James. John versus Matthew. Law versus grace. But if all Scripture is God-breathed (2 Tim. 3:16), then all Scripture harmonizes. God does not disagree with himself. He is not the author of confusion. He does not grow in understanding or shift with time. And because of that, his Word is not scattered across different human agendas. Instead, it is bound together by divine authorship.

This changes how we interpret everything. If God inspired all of it, then Leviticus and Revelation are not in tension. Neither are the Gospels and the Epistles. Paul does not disagree with James on how one goes about gaining eternal life. Any interpretation that pits one part of Scripture against another is necessarily flawed. It has misunderstood something. The correct reading is always the one in which the full counsel of God holds together without strain. And that means we must read Scripture with Scripture. The Bible must be interpreted in light of the rest of Scripture. It is not a puzzle to be solved by modern eyes looking for hidden meanings. Rather, it is a revelation designed to be understood in context, both literary and canonical. Too often interpreters only engage with the direct context. But if Scripture is truly God's Word, then any interpretation needs to be firmly rooted in the whole of the canon.

Jesus affirmed this when he said, "Scripture cannot be broken" (John 10:35). The whole testimony of Scripture is unbreakable. You cannot cut it into pieces and treat one part as true while sidelining the rest. Jesus consistently appealed to the entirety of God's Word, not just isolated prooftexts, to show that all of it pointed to him. The Law, the Prophets, the Psalms, they all spoke in unison because they all shared the same Author and pointed toward Jesus. He also used various passages, even heavily disputed ones today, to make points for what he was saying. What Jesus taught was what Scripture teaches.

The apostles followed the same pattern. Peter wrote that "no prophecy of Scripture comes from someone's own interpretation" but that "men spoke from God as they were carried along by the Holy Spirit" (2 Peter 1:20–21). Paul insisted that what he taught was not man's wisdom but the very words taught by the Spirit (1 Cor. 2:13). Scripture was meant to express consistent truths about God and how he interacts with the world. That is why we are commanded to "rightly divide" the Word, not creatively reinterpret it. Since God, via his Word, speaks with one voice, we are expected to hear it rightly and follow it fully.

This also means that our theological conclusions must never rest on isolated passages. If your doctrine relies on a handful of verses that appear to stand alone, especially if those verses seem to be in tension with the rest of Scripture, you've likely missed the point. The true doctrine is the one that can be found, confirmed, and explained through the entire biblical witness. Truth is revealed progressively in the Bible, but never contradictorily. God's later words illuminate his earlier ones. They do not override them.

The unity of Scripture is one of the most powerful proofs of its divine origin. No other sacred text in history carries this level of internal cohesion. Try stitching together the spiritual ideas of roughly forty authors across fifteen hundred years and you'll get contradiction, confusion, and chaos, even if they are all writing on the same topic. Yet Scripture both avoids this and demonstrates continuity from Genesis to Revelation. The same God who creates in Genesis is the one who judges in Revelation. The covenant made with Abraham is fulfilled in Christ. The promises of the prophets come to life in the Gospels. There is no way that this came about by chance, nor is it possible for all of the authors to have done this without divine intervention. God *must* have been directly involved in the writing of the Scriptures.

Overall, if Scripture is true, then every verse is not merely compatible with the others, it *depends* on the others. The Bible is not a collection of theological options. It is the self-revelation of God, speaking in one voice across every book, every passage, every line. If you want to hear the truth, you must be willing to hear *all* of it.

Summary

This chapter shifts from the philosophical foundations of truth to its biblical expression, arguing that Scripture presents truth as singular, exclusive, and authoritative. Jesus' claim to be "the truth" (John 14:6) is not metaphorical but a categorical declaration that he alone reveals God and provides salvation. The Bible repeatedly asserts the uniqueness of God, the exclusivity of salvation through Christ, and the singular authority of its teachings. This exclusivity applies not only to salvation but to all doctrines—marriage, gender, sin, and more—leaving no room for relativism or doctrinal compromise. Scripture speaks with one voice because it has one divine Author, meaning no part of the Bible contradicts another. Therefore, sound doctrine must harmonize with the whole biblical witness, rejecting interpretations that isolate verses or pit them against each other. Ultimately, allegiance to God means accepting the exclusivity of his truth in every matter he addresses.

Discussion Questions:

Summarize this chapter in your own words.

How does Jesus' statement in John 14:6 challenge the modern assumption that multiple religious paths can lead to God?

Why is it important to interpret individual passages in light of the entire biblical canon? Can you think of examples where neglecting this principle leads to error?

What practical differences would it make in the church if all believers treated "secondary" doctrines with the same seriousness as "primary" ones?

In what ways does our culture's preference for inclusivity and tolerance conflict with the Bible's exclusive claims, and how should Christians respond?

How does recognizing Scripture as God's unified, inerrant Word influence the way you respond to passages that challenge your personal views or lifestyle?

If you were teaching or discipling others, how would you help them see the connection between God's unity, the exclusivity of Christ, and the singular truth of Scripture?

Chapter Four

Truth vs. Perspective: A Look at Contextual Truths

Since the most common views today tend to be relativistic (moral, religious, or otherwise), even within Christianity, it is necessary to demonstrate how relativism fails. This chapter will move from a discussion of opinion, perspective, and truth to engaging with common relativist phrases. Toward the end, we will look at how, via context, some form of relativism does exist, but it is vastly different than it is typically argued, and it *still* fits the idea that there is only *one* truth for each and every topic or question.

Opinion, Perspective, and Truth

Before we begin dismantling the most common relativist slogans, we need to establish a basic framework. Much of the confusion surrounding truth today stems from people not understanding the difference between *opinion*, *perspective*, and *truth*. These are not interchangeable terms and conflating them leads to significant problems. The modern world thrives on ambiguity in these categories, and sadly, the church has too often followed suit. But if we're going to talk about truth, especially biblical truth, we must define our terms with precision.

An *opinion* is a personal judgment, often based on feelings or preferences. Saying "I like blue better than green" is an opinion. It might be true that you feel that way, but it's a claim about your internal state, not about the world. *Perspective*, on the other hand, is the vantage point from which something is observed. Perspectives can reveal parts of the truth, but they are not the truth in themselves. You may see one side of a building while I see the other, but the building remains what it is regardless of how we view it. Truth is what *is* (i.e., what actually corresponds to reality). It is not limited to how we feel or what we can see. While all truth needs context to be understood properly, objective or universal truths are those that are true regardless of one's tastes or preferences. An example would be: Provided that the laws of physics are still in effect, humans cannot walk on water.

The problem arises when people confuse their opinion or perspective with objective, universal truth itself. This is where relativism finds its foothold. When someone says, "Well, that's just how I see it," or "That's true for me," they're collapsing truth into preference. But Scripture doesn't do this. Scripture speaks authoritatively about the nature of God, salvation, sin, morality, and the created world. It does not leave room for competing truth claims to peacefully coexist. If two claims contradict each other, at least one of them is false or, as we will see later, the context is different, allowing two seemingly contradictory statements to coexist.

That said, not everything we encounter is absolute in the same way. All statements are dependent on context, but some are also dependent on *conditions* (which is a specific type of context), particularly those involving human preference, taste, or feeling. These are real truths, but they are *contextual*, not universal. Saying "I hate pineapple on pizza" is a true statement about me, not about pizza itself. The truth there is contingent upon my current preferences. How this works is the subject of the rest of this chapter.

In what follows, we'll look at several popular relativist phrases and demonstrate how each one falls apart under scrutiny. Some of them stem from secular assumptions, while others have infiltrated the church. Either way, they must be challenged, because when we lose clarity on what truth is, we begin to accept contradiction, celebrate disagreement, and abandon our commitment to rightly divide the Word of truth. And once that happens, doctrine becomes a matter of taste, and taste is no foundation for objective, universal truth.

Common Relativist Phrases

While there are many more, what follows is a brief engagement with the most common relativist phrases. Some of these are used by secularists while others happen within religious or Christian circles.

That's True for You but Not for Me

Another way of putting this phrase is, "You have your truth, and I have mine." Either way, this relativistic phrase has problems. When it comes to universal truth claims, there are no examples where the truth is different for someone else. Below, we will examine whether or not there are subjective or relativistic things as a nuance to what I am saying here.

Regardless of which way one wants to phrase this statement, it's utter nonsense despite sounding nice and tolerant. Truth doesn't change based on who believes it. If Jesus rose from the dead, that's true for everyone, whether they accept it or not. Saying "that's your truth" confuses personal preference with objective reality. Preferences are real, but they're not truth in the biblical or philosophical sense. Truth is singular, exclusive, and unchanging (unless tethered to something that is inherently unstable like one's taste buds). If two claims contradict each other, one is false. Period. Truth doesn't flex to fit our feelings. It just is. Even truths that are based on something subjective (i.e., your taste buds), still have only one, objective truth statement attached to them as we will see later in this chapter.

All Religions Basically Teach the Same Thing

This slogan is common enough to even be the subject

of whole books.[1] The phrase "all religions basically teach the same thing" is a common refrain in contemporary culture, often promoted in the name of tolerance or unity. This idea, known as *simple religious pluralism*, claims that Islam, Mormonism, Hinduism, Christianity, and other faiths are equally valid paths to God. But this perspective not only ignores the vast contradictions between these systems, it also completely undermines the unique claims of Christianity and of Jesus himself.

Simple pluralism, like relativism, asserts that no one religion can claim exclusive truth. Yet this collapses under logical scrutiny. If all religions are true, then the exclusive truth-claims made by many of them (especially Christianity) must also be true, which is logically impossible. As Paul Gould, Travis Dickinson, and Keith Loftin note, "The view [simple religious pluralism] literally collapses under its own logical weight."[2]

Moreover, religious pluralism demands that Jesus' clear and repeated claims to exclusivity be dismissed or reinterpreted. But this is intellectually dishonest. We cannot accept Jesus as a great teacher while rejecting his most

---

1. See, for example, *Do Christians, Muslims, and Jews Worship the Same God? Four Views* edited by Ronnie P. Campbell and Christopher Gnanakan. This book technically is less about the view that all religions are functionally the same than it is about the philosophical problem that, under classical metaphysics, the three major monotheistic religions all worship the same God. That said, the problem is essentially the same, it is just more philosophical than religious relativism typically espouses.

2. Gould, *Stand Firm*, 130.

definitive teachings. If Jesus is the only way to God, as he said, then any system that denies this claim cannot lead to the same God.

In reality, religions do not teach the same thing. They make radically different claims about God, salvation, sin, truth, and the afterlife. The attempt to merge them into a unified whole results not in clarity or peace, but in confusion and distortion. Biblical Christianity stands apart, not because it seeks division, but because truth is, by its nature, exclusive.

That's Just Your Interpretation

This idea is probably the most troubling as it comes from fellow believers. The idea behind the phrase, "That's just your interpretation" is that there are multiple ways (potentially an infinite number of ways if taken to an extreme) in which a given passage can truthfully be interpreted. It is the expression of relativism as it has been accepted by the church. The problem is that there are *not* multiple equally valid ways to interpret a given passage. This is a basic hermeneutical principle. A passage has one correct interpretation and a myriad of *applications* depending on the context the interpreter is in. Now, it may not be *easy* to find the correct interpretation, especially if there is some amount of textual problems. Nor are we guaranteed to *like* the correct interpretation.

Preference Is Real but
Not Equivalent to the Truth

Now that we've clarified what truth is—and established
that there is only one true statement about any given question in life or faith—it's fair to ask: *Does this mean that
nothing is relative?*

Believe it or not, there *are* things that are relative. But
I don't mean "relative" in the way relativists use the term,
where everyone's personal opinion magically becomes true
for them and must be accepted by others no matter how
irrational. That's subjectivity pretending to be something
it's not.

Instead of using "relative" though, due to its connotations, the better way to say it is this: Some truths are
perspective-based. They are still real truths, but they're only
true *within a particular context*. This is obviously seen in
scenarios based on taste.

Let me illustrate with something simple. Pizza has
an objective truth claim. While there may be some debate
about the exact boundaries of what counts as a pizza, we
can probably agree on this much: A pizza is a flatbread
with sauce, cheese, and often various toppings. It's usually
round and it's edible. That's enough to define it for our
purposes here.

Now, here's where *perspective* comes in. My wife loves
pepperoni and pineapple on her pizza. I, on the other hand,
think pineapple on pizza is an abomination. We split piz-
zas—half has pineapple, while the other half does not. But

somehow, pineapple juice still creeps onto my half. It's sweet. It's fruity. It's horribly *wrong* (my pizza shouldn't be sweet or fruity!). Still, I can't deny that her half is *technically* pizza. It fits the objective criteria. But whether or not it *tastes good*? That's based on perspective. It's not an objective claim about the nature of pizza, but a subjective claim about my experience of it. That said, despite it being a subjective claim, there is still an objective truth claim within the subjective one. We will engage this in a moment.

This same structure applies all over life, including in how people respond to God. God is real, and he is who Scripture reveals him to be. If what I just said is true, then that's not up for debate. But people are absolutely allowed to dislike that truth. They may find it offensive, restrictive, or frightening. Their reaction doesn't change the reality of who God is, but it does change how they relate to that reality, which is itself a truth about them.

Another example is the Flat Earth Theory. Many people today believe the Earth is flat. Just because they *believe it*, though, does not mean it is true. There is an abundance of evidence that demonstrates that the Earth is spherical. Rejecting this does not magically make one's beliefs true. Whether flat-earthers want to admit it or not, how they interact with the world depends on the Earth being spherical. They may not *like* that, but it is true anyway.

So yes, subjectivity exists, but only in domains where it makes sense. Preference, taste, and feeling are contextual categories. They aren't lies, nor are they false. However, they aren't universal either.

Even preference-based truths still obey the rule of *one truth per context*. To me, pineapple on pizza is disgusting. To my wife, it's culinary perfection. These are both true and they're not contradictory even if the "to me" and "to my wife" contexts were only implied. They don't make the same claim from the same reference point.

Here's why this matters: Preferences change. And when preferences change, the truth about those preferences changes too. This is because the context (the preference) is no longer the same. Thus, the *truth claim* about the preference must change.

I used to think a burger with anything but cheese was an excellent way to ruin a good burger. Just meat, cheese, and a bun, anything else was gross. But over time, my preferences shifted, and now, I enjoy burgers loaded with mayo, onions, lettuce, pickles, and jalapeños.

The truth about my burger preferences had to change—*not because truth itself changed*, but because *the condition of my preferences changed*.

That's the difference: Truth remains one per frame. But some truths are tethered to changing (conditional) frames. The truth of my preferences aligns with the current reality of said preferences. When the preference changes, so does the truth about the preference.

Contextual Truths in Relation to God

We see this in Scripture all the time. X will happen provided that you do Y. It also shows how current reality is conditional. So long as the universe exists, gravity exists (and is constant), oxygen is real and necessary for life, and the sun exists (though the sun could disappear before the universe does). But Scripture says reality as we know it will "pass away." No longer will we need the sun and the moon to light the sky. *God* will light the sky (Revelation 21:23). Thus, even our current universal truths about the universe are subject to change if the universe, the frame, ceases to be.

Summary

This chapter critiques relativism by distinguishing between opinion, perspective, and truth. Opinions are personal judgments based on feelings or preferences; perspectives are limited vantage points; truth is that which corresponds to reality. Relativism blurs these distinctions, reducing truth to personal preference and allowing contradictory claims to coexist. The author engages with common relativist slogans such as "That's true for you but not for me," "All religions basically teach the same thing," and "That's just your interpretation," demonstrating their logical and biblical flaws. The text acknowledges that some truths are conditional, while insisting that even these obey the principle of one truth per context. Changing contexts (e.g., shifting preferences) change the truth claim, not truth itself. The chapter closes by affirming that Scripture recognizes conditional truths and future changes to reality, but these changes are anchored in the constancy of God's truth.

Discussion Questions:

Summarize this chapter in your own words.

In your own words, how would you explain the difference between an opinion, a perspective, and truth? Why is it important not to confuse these categories in theological or moral discussions?

The author argues that relativism collapses under logical and biblical scrutiny. What are some examples from your own experience where "that's true for you but not for me" has been used, and how could you respond biblically?

How does the claim that "all religions basically teach the same thing" fail both logically and theologically? What dangers might arise in the church if such thinking is accepted?

The phrase "That's just your interpretation" is addressed as a form of relativism within the church. How can believers approach biblical interpretation in a way that seeks the one correct meaning while still respecting legitimate differences in application?

The author distinguishes between universal truths and conditional truths, such as personal tastes or preferences. Can you think of examples from your life where the context changed and the truth about your preference changed with it?

Scripture contains conditional statements about reality ("If you do X, then Y will happen"). How can understanding these conditional truths help us better interpret God's promises and warnings?

CHAPTER FIVE

WHY CHRISTIANS DISAGREE

ONE THING THAT HAS been immediately obvious to pretty much everyone is that Christians do *not* agree on everything. In fact, given the proclivity of Christians to divide over doctrine and create new denominations, we seem to be a prime example of those who *should* be unified but are clearly not. If my original argument that there is one and only one fully accurate truth statement about any given topic or question is true, why do we have so many different interpretations of Scripture? In other words, why do we have so many debated doctrines in Christianity if my truth claim is accurate? All of the most hotly debated topics in Christianity such as women in ministry, old versus young earth creationism, Calvinism versus Arminianism, etc. have *one* option that is the full truth and nothing but the truth. At least, that is my claim. Many would argue that the truth of these debates and topics cannot be fully known as Scripture is not clear on said topics and that one's position comes down to how Scripture is interpreted. I would fundamentally disagree with that. But if I am correct in saying that each of these doctrines has exactly one truth statement, how can we go about determining which view is correct, or whether there needs to be a third option? Below, I will address three kinds of doctrinal debates and how we can go about trying to solve them.

Authority Confusion

The first category is one in which Christians can relatively easily determine the correct path. In this type of debate, one side holds Scripture as supreme while the other side holds something as equal to or above Scripture. One of the most common examples of this is the old earth versus young earth debate. Only *one* side holds to the supremacy of Scripture over everything else. Every other view takes something foreign to the text of Scripture and uses it to interpret Scripture. In this case, it is contemporary science. Any version of old earth creationism involves accepting modern science as being correct, at least regarding the claim that the Earth is old. Thus, old earth creationists need to reinterpret passages of Scripture to better align with the scientific consensus. On the other hand, young earth creationism holds Scripture as supreme and interprets *scientific* findings through the lens of Scripture. This style of debate should be very easy for Christians to see the correct side. Scripture is our authority. Therefore, the side that emphasizes Scripture is likely the side that holds to the truth or is closest to it.[1]

What is not so easy about this category is that it includes theological tradition as being a confusion of authority. Tradition is all well and good... as long as it aligns with Scripture. This gets twisted more than we would like to think. What I will not dispute is that doctrine as we know it developed. Humans took the biblical evidence and tried to synthesize it in a way that made sense. Everyone either attempts to create doctrine (or at least refine it) or they simply uphold what has been passed along to them. The Roman Catholic Church and the Orthodox Church both have catechized this process by saying that God has given the church the means to do this doctrinal construction. As such, they place tradition on par with Scripture. Even many Protestants move in these circles. The assumption in Protestantism is that God wouldn't allow his church to develop false doctrine and therefore the tradition, especially early tradition is untouchable. For example, Michael Bird writes, "Evangelical theologians, who claim to be biblical and orthodox, are not at liberty to dispense with eternal generation."[2] Eternal generation is the idea that the Son is constantly being generated by the Father. This is how the historical church has typically attempted to differentiate

---

1. This debate is handled in much more detail in chapters 10 and 11 of my book *Contending for the Truth: A Biblical Look at Thirteen Contentious Doctrines*.

2. Michael F. Bird and Scott Harrower, eds, *Trinity without Hierarchy: Reclaiming Nicene Orthodoxy in Evangelical Theology* (Grand Rapids, MI: Kregel Academic, 2019), 13.

between the Father and the Son. The problem is that this idea, that the Son is *eternally* begotten (generated), is not to be found in Scripture. Its origin is philosophy. God *must* be like "A". Therefore, when Scripture says "B," it really means "A". A similar move is made regarding the Spirit. In the tradition, the contention that the Spirit eternally proceeds from the Father and Son. This is only defensible philosophically. Scripture does not teach it. Scripture *does* teach that the Spirit proceeds from the Father and Son at a *specific point in time* (John 15:26). Many Christians do not even realize that what they believe may not be biblical. It is simply what has been handed down to them.

I only critiqued science and theological tradition in this section; however, it needs to be noted that almost *anything* can become the root of authority confusion. Emotions, reason, preferences, etc., can all become problematic if they are given authority over Scripture and truth. In some ways, this makes authority confusion the "umbrella" category that the others fall under. Nor does acknowledging that Scripture needs to be *the* go-to authority mean that other things like tradition and science do not have value. They simply can't be used to trump Scripture.

Interpretive Imbalance

The second type of debate is when both sides have "their" Scripture verses. We see this in the Calvinism versus Arminianism debate, specifically their views on the doctrine of election. Both sides have a significant number of verses that they use to support their assertions. The problem is that both sets of verses *contradict* each other, at least when used separately. One of the most important things to know about Scripture is that it cannot contradict itself. Due to space limitations, I am not going to defend that statement here.[3] If two verses seem to contradict each other, we need to find out how they fit together in a non-contradictory way. In the case of Calvinism versus Arminianism, we see two seemingly contradictory sets of verses. On the one hand, Calvinism points out that God's sovereignty is everything. TULIP, for example, entirely hinges on God's sovereignty.[4] If God is sovereign in the way Calvinism points out, then TULIP is true. He chooses who will come to him apart from any choice on the part of humans. Those in the Reformed tradition have many verses to back this up. On the other hand, Arminianism points out all the verses that show that humans have the ability, the free will, to choose to follow God, often to a fault.[5] Again, they have a large number of verses to support this view. The problem is that, as argued, these two ideas completely disagree with one another. Since each side is using Scripture, this means that Scripture is contradictory, or at least appears to be

---

3. See my short book, *The Inerrancy of Scripture: An Overview and Defense* for a brief but pointed academic defense of this doctrine.

4. TULIP stands for Total depravity, Unconditional election, Limited atonement, Irresistible grace, and Perseverance of the saints.

5. Roger E. Olson, *Arminian Theology: Myths and Realities* (Downers Grove, IL: InterVarsity Press, 2006), 97-98.

in debates like this. When we focus on one set of verses too much, doctrinal debates become falsely dichotomized. Often, the truth is not in picking a team, but in digging deeper and asking more precise questions. A failure to seek theological *nuance* often leaves us defending caricatures instead of contending for truth.

Prophetic Incompleteness or Lack of Robust Biblical Evidence

The third reason Christians disagree can be summed up by the idea that, sometimes, we simply do not have all of the necessary information to be able to provide an accurate truth claim. To put this another way, for a Christian, the question is not whether there *is* a single truth about each topic or question; rather it is whether we have the necessary *information* to determine what the truth statement is. Going back to the water example Chapter 1, if I were not present to be able to tell someone that the cup of water is half full, they would have a 50/50 chance of getting the answer right but would have no way of knowing if they were right. We can look for clues on the glass to try to figure it out (such as lip marks or water droplets on the side of the cup to see if it has been drunk or poured out), but we can never know *for sure* unless we are present when the drink is poured or drunk or if we are told by the person who made the drink.

Likewise, knowledge about God and his Word can come with doubt as to whether we are correct or can even know we are correct. Though I would argue that this is rarer than many make it out to be, there are legitimate examples. One major example is anything regarding end-times prophecies. We can dissect the passages that talk about the end times as much as we want and we might even come to the correct conclusions; however, we have no way of knowing *for sure* that is the correct conclusion until the end comes unless Scripture is abundantly clear. For example, the rapture is a doctrine of Scripture we can be sure will happen despite the general bent to disbelieve in it today. Plenty of Scriptural evidence supports the fact that Christians will be "caught up" to meet Jesus. That the rapture will happen is actually not up for debate. That said, the *timing* of the rapture is. I personally believe that Scripture most readily teaches a pretribulation rapture. *However*, there is potential room for a later rapture if there is a big enough distinction between the pouring out of the bowls of God's wrath which begins in Revelation 16 and the rest of the wrath found in Revelation. I do not believe that this potential is significant, but it is there. Thus, I would argue that it is best to hold to a pretribulation rapture while doing so loosely enough to not damage our faith if it does not end up happening as expected. That said, I could be wrong even though I see no truly valid argument for a time later than a pretribulation rapture. If you want to see more about my view on this, I engage this topic directly in *Tribulation as Wrath: Rethinking the Timing of God's Judgment*. The fact is that we will not know for sure the timing of the rapture until *after* it happens. Does this mean that we should not study the end times and come to conclusions regarding it? Of course not! Scripture is clear: We are to be ready and eagerly long for Jesus' second coming.[6] We cannot be ready for it if we have no idea what to expect or what to look for. Thus, we *need* to study the signs of the times.

Another example would be Paul's thorn in the flesh (2 Corinthians 12:7). We know it existed, we know it was a problem for Paul, we know it was described as a "messenger from Satan," and it was also of benefit to him (by keeping him humble). However, what it is *exactly* is never given to us. Nor are we told precisely how it accomplished its mission. This is a non-future case that demonstrates that there *are* examples where we do not have all of the required information to be overly specific. At best, we can claim what I laid out initially. Paul did indeed have a "thorn in the flesh". To go beyond what is laid out explicitly in the text is to dive straight into speculation. It isn't a bad thing to speculate on this. That said, if one's speculation leads to a dogmatic view of exactly what it could or could not be, then the speculation has gone too far.

Preference Elevated to Principle

In the previous chapter, we looked at how preference has a truth claim to it, but that it is subjective to the person who holds the preference. So long as this *remains* subjective to

---

6. Wayne Grudem, *Systematic Theology: An Introduction to Biblical Doctrine* (Grand Rapids, MI: Zondervan Academic, 2020), 1344-45.

the person, it is completely fine. Unfortunately, it is often the case that believers will fight like crazy to try and change things that are subjective. Sometimes this is about the style of music or even the color of the carpet. I can hate the color of the carpet in my church, but that doesn't mean I should try to force my subjective truth (it is true only to *me*) on the rest of the church. Fighting over these kinds of things has literally caused church splits. In such cases, the church split for frivolous reasons. Subjective truths are real truths, but they have a specific context and, outside of said context, they are not true.

Another practical example would be homeschooling. I know Christians who would argue that you can't be a Christian if you aren't homeschooling your kids. While I generally agree that our public school system is broken and personally feel convicted to homeschool my own kids, it goes too far to say that a Christian *must* homeschool. A case can be made to say that homeschooling is objectively better at the current stage in history, but a blanket claim that homeschooling is the only way a Christian can faithfully raise their kids is going too far. Biblically, we don't have the grounds to state this. In biblical times, the family *was* responsible for the training of their kids, but they also had to go to school via the synagogues. Parents are still responsible for raising our kids well, but that can mean different things based on the specific goals of the parents. If you homeschool your kids, you gain direct input into what they learn; however, it also means that you are expected to be able to do so to a high level. Some families don't have the ability or the luxury of homeschooling. On the other hand, public schools and many private schools are valid options. The challenge with them is that, intentional or not, they often seek to instill a different value system into our kids, and they are generalized education. Everyone is pretty much taught to the same level. Thus, Christian parents need to realize that public schooling their children will bring its own set of problems that the parents need to be ready to deal with. Essentially, whether parents homeschool or not, they are responsible for the proper upbringing of their children into the Lord and as solid members of society. Telling someone they can't be a Christian if they don't homeschool their kids is elevating a preference, or even a real conviction from God for *your* family, to the level of principle.

Dealing With the Above Problems

The four problems outlined above demonstrate why Christians do not agree on a whole host of doctrines, but what can we do about it? Below is a brief engagement with ways to solve these problems. The next chapter will focus more on *how* one should go about discovering truth, especially as it relates to God and his Word.

Scripture Is King

As believers, our final authority must always be the Word of God. If any source, whether science, philosophy, tradition, or emotion, seems to conflict with Scripture, it is that source that must be reevaluated, not Scripture. God's Word is perfect (Psalm 19:7), unbreakable (John 10:35), and sufficient (2 Tim. 3:16–17). Without this conviction, theological coherence collapses. No claim from Scripture can be trusted and something *else* needs to become the arbiter of truth found in Scripture (i.e., one's ability to reason, science, tradition, etc.).[7]

Scripture Cannot Contradict Itself

Because Scripture is breathed out by God, it cannot contain contradiction. If two passages appear to teach opposing ideas, the error is in our interpretation, not in the text. Sound theology comes from harmonizing what all of Scripture says, not privileging one verse or passage at the expense of another (Acts 20:27). The idea that Scripture cannot contradict itself is the logical conclusion of the ideas that Scripture is inerrant (without error) and infallible (without the possibility of failing). If these two ideas are true of Scripture, then it is impossible for Scripture to contradict itself as it can neither fail, nor does it contain error. A real contradiction in the text would be fundamentally opposed to either of those terms. For sake of space, I will not defend the inerrancy or infallibility of Scripture here. However, I have published a short work precisely on this topic.[8]

---

7. Stephen L. Andrew, "Biblical Inerrancy," *Chafer Theological Seminary Journal* 8.1 (Winter 2002): 17. Andrew argues that most uphold reason as the arbiter of truth when inerrancy is rejected.

8. L. J. Anderson, *The Inerrancy of Scripture: An Overview and Defense* (Billings, MT: Lamad Press, 2025).

Harmonization, Not Cherry-Picking, Is the Way Forward

In the interpretive imbalance section above, I said that debates like the Calvinism vs. Arminianism one need to account for theological nuance. To put this another way, a nuanced view on the doctrine of election must take into account both sets of verses and see how they fit together. As it stands, Scripture is contradictory under the current debate due to the overemphasis of certain passages of Scripture. Since Scripture cannot contradict itself, as we saw in the last section, this simply cannot be the case. Instead, we need to look for how these sets of verses mesh together. Essentially, these verses need to meet in the middle somehow. My personal explanation for this particular debate is that God, being sovereign, has ordained the *way* to come back to him and has called all humans to turn away from their sins and follow him, but we then have the choice as to whether we will choose his way. This view allows for both God's sovereignty and human free will to play a distinct role in a person's salvation, which is important because, again, there are plenty of verses that support both sides of this.[9] We don't get to pick and choose which verses we will use. We need to align ourselves with what Scripture teaches. If Scripture seems to be saying something different from what we believe, even if said belief is held by millions of Christians around the world, we need to seriously examine

---

9. For a more in-depth look at this debate, see my book *Contending for the Truth: A Biblical Look at Thirteen Contentious Doctrines* chapter 13.

that belief in light of Scripture. Let Scripture teach us. These types of debates often have a correct interpretation somewhere in the middle of the two opposing views which is a nuanced form of the debate.

Deep Study Paired with Humility

Finding the truth in life and in Scripture resembles a crime scene investigation. We need to find as much relevant evidence as we can and try to piece them together as coherently as they can be pieced together. The challenges that we face in this are varied. As laid out above, many times we have certain presuppositions that directly conflict with our ability to understand the pieces properly. In other words, we bring intellectual baggage to the metaphorical crime scene. If a crime scene investigator goes into the crime scene with a preconceived notion of what went down, they are liable to let that be the lens through which they filter the entire crime scene. Other times, we don't *have* all the relevant pieces of the puzzle. In which case, we need to realize that, sometimes, the answer to a question we have is, "I don't know," or "my best guess is 'X'". The point is to remain humble and thus to remain teachable, which leads directly into the next section.

Kill Your Pride

Pride is at once a good thing and yet it is also incredibly dangerous. It is not inherently evil to have pride in one's work, children, God, or whatever else one might feel prideful about. The danger is that it can be both blinding and damaging. When it comes to understanding God and his Word, it is important for us to stand firmly on what we believe while maintaining teachability. Odds are extremely good that neither you, nor I, are perfect in our understanding of God. Even with specific doctrines, we should expect to need to constantly refine our position. Unfortunately, that can't happen if we hold so strongly to our beliefs that nothing anyone says, even if that someone is Scripture, can sway our belief. It means that, instead of being iron sharpening iron (Proverbs 27:17) when we come together and discuss theology, we just slam against each other like two fully hardened swords hoping the other will break under the weight of our arguments. All the while, we steadfastly refuse to think through what the other people are saying. To fix this, we need to kill our pride and realize that we might be wrong. Even when we can say with confidence that something is true, there is almost certainly room for improvement in our understanding. Let that knowledge temper your pride.

From a similar angle, pride causes problems with our ability to repent (to change one's mind about something). A pastor who has held a certain doctrinal position for fifty years is likely going to have some level of pride in that position. After all, they have taught others the same thing throughout all of those years. But what if they are wrong on their position? Pride often won't allow them to change their mind. It won't allow them to repent. However, if that pastor keeps their pride in check, they are positioned in a way that they can actually say, "I was wrong, and here's why." It is powerful to see someone like that look at Scripture or hear an argument against their position and realize that their position no longer holds water. That is the kind of example Christians should have when it comes to truth, especially Christians who are in leadership positions.

Summary

This chapter argues that while there is only one correct truth statement for every theological question, Christians disagree for four main reasons. The first is authority confusion, which occurs when something other than Scripture—such as science, tradition, emotion, or personal reasoning—is treated as equal to or above God's Word. The second is interpretive imbalance, where individuals emphasize certain passages over others, creating false dichotomies, as in the Calvinism versus Arminianism debate. The third is prophetic incompleteness, which happens when Scripture does not provide enough information to reach a definitive conclusion, as in the timing of the rapture or the nature of Paul's thorn in the flesh. The fourth is the elevation of personal preference to principle, where subjective convictions are imposed on others as though they were universal biblical mandates. To address these problems, the author stresses the need to uphold Scripture as the supreme authority, affirm that it cannot contradict itself, harmonize rather than cherry-pick passages, study deeply with humility, and kill pride so that believers remain teachable and willing to change their minds when confronted with the truth.

Discussion Questions:

Summarize this chapter in your own words.

How can we practically identify when an authority other than Scripture is subtly influencing our interpretation?

In what ways might theological tradition be both beneficial and dangerous to doctrinal accuracy?

What methods can help reconcile seemingly contradictory passages without dismissing one side?

How should Christians approach doctrines where Scripture does not give full clarity, especially on future events?

What safeguards can prevent personal preferences from being elevated to universal principles in church life?

How can humility and teachability be cultivated in leaders who have held firm doctrinal positions for decades?

CHAPTER SIX

HOW TO DISCOVER THE TRUTH (WITHOUT FALLING INTO ERROR)

S O FAR IN THIS book, I have argued there is only one correct interpretation of any passage. That interpretation may have multiple layers or even multiple points but, even in cases like this, there is only one fully true interpretation of that passage.[1] That may sound harsh to a culture steeped in subjectivity, but reality is not shaped by our feelings. Interestingly, many Christians would try to fit this

---

1. See, for example, Kenneth Berding and Jonathan Lunde, eds., *Three Views on the New Testament Use of the Old Testament* (Grand Rapids: Zondervan, 2007). In this book, all three of the contributors (Darrell Bock, Walter Kaiser, and Peter Enns) all hold that verses can contain different "meanings," especially regarding Old Testament uses of a verse versus the New Testament usage of the same verse, but they have varied ways of showing this. Contextual Absolutism argues in verses like Hosea 11:1 (quoted in Matthew 2:15), two meanings are meant by the author and both need to be upheld as the *one* meaning of the verse. Both Israel *and* Christ are sons who were called "out of Egypt". To say it only referred to Israel is incomplete. To say it only refers to Christ is also incomplete.

idea under "applications".[2] Thus, the passage in the first footnote of this chapter (Hosea 11:1) can only be said to be about Israel, but it *applies* to Jesus. However, that assumes that God did not intend Hosea 11:1 to *be* a refence to Christ as well as to Israel and instead posits that Jesus took the passage out of context and applied it to himself... which goes directly against Protestant hermeneutics. We are never to take something out of its context and say it applies to us in that way. To solve this, I would argue, via Contextual Absolutism, that God intended Hosea 11:1 to have two meanings, one regarding Israel and one regarding Christ. Thus, a correct interpretation of Hosea 11:1 necessarily includes both meanings. In other words, there is only *one* fully correct interpretation, even when a passage can have multiple legitimate referents.

Before moving on, I want to make something clear. There *is* only one correct interpretation of any given passage, even acknowledging that the interpretation might have multiple layers. That said, *applications* for a passage are abundant. One can apply the truth of a passage to any number of valid situations. It is part of what makes Scripture so valuable. All of the new things we have seen in the modern age can still have the truths of Scripture applied to

---

2. Robert L. Thomas, "Biblical Hermeneutics: Single Meaning and Its Effects," paper presented at the Chafer Conference, *The Master's Seminary*, 2009, accessed August 12, 2025, https://www.deanbible.org/dbmfiles/notes/2009-ChaferConf-Thomas-Paper-02.pdf.

them even if Scripture does not directly address the topic.[3] This is a well-known hermeneutical idea. Robert Thomas (cited above) demonstrates that quite clearly even if he ultimately disagrees with my claim that multiple meanings can fit under one correct interpretation. The difference between a passage having multiple applications and a passage having multiple referents, is that applications apply the principles found in the passage while the words themselves cannot be directly applied unless that is what the author (both human and divine) meant.

When it comes to interpreting Scripture, the pursuit of truth demands more than sincerity. It demands discipline. Interpretation is not a personal art form or a matter of devotional creativity. It is an act of discovery, which requires rules, and these rules are not arbitrary. They arise from the nature of Scripture itself. If the Bible is inerrant, then it is internally consistent. If it is God-breathed, then it reflects the character of God. He is not the author of confusion, and his Word does not speak with two voices. It says what he meant it to say, as clearly as God wanted to say it.

So then, we must read it with integrity and seek to build our biblical literacy, something all Christians should

---

3. Look at the previous chapter's engagement with homeschooling as an example.

aspire toward.[4] That means we must apply consistent principles of interpretation. This chapter outlines five: Scripture interprets Scripture. Logical consistency matters. No
verse cancels another. Emotion and tradition must not
override context. And finally, truth requires both discipline
and humility. These are actually a form of presupposition.[5]
Many argue that no one comes to Scripture without presuppositions, likely correctly.[6] However, many assume that
presuppositions are inherently *bad*. This is not the case.
Presuppositions can range from bad to good and anywhere
in between. This is something that is real while often un-
acknowledged. For example, "The Chicago Statement on
Biblical Inerrancy" states, "We affirm that canonical Scripture should always be interpreted on the basis that it is

---

4. Kevin J. Vanhoozer, *Mere Christian Hermeneutics: Transfiguring What
It Means to Read the Bible Theologically* (Grand Rapids, MI: Zondervan
Academic, 2024), 29. While acknowledging that Christians have never really agreed on how to interpret the Bible, Vanhoozer wrote this
hermeneutics book for those who "care about biblical literacy" and those
who are "puzzled about the nature and method of literal interpretation."
Arguably, being literate in the Bible and being able to apply a consistent,
literal interpretation that rightly accounts for genre, idioms, and the like,
should be the goal of any Christian. This includes the theological level
where we are to take the seemingly disparate facts of Scripture and build
them into a cohesive whole.

5. A presupposition is something that must be true for the conclusion to
follow logically but does not necessarily need to be defined at the outset
of the argument.

6. See, for example, John C. Peckham, *The Love of God: A Canonical Model*
(Downers Grove, IL: InterVarsity Press, 2015), 46-47.

infallible and inerrant."[7] That is bringing a presupposition to the text of Scripture, which isn't inherently bad. In fact, I would agree with the statement. The danger with presuppositions is that they can be hidden. *Bad* presuppositions, then, negatively affect one's interpretation of Scripture. Below, you will find five presuppositions that should be brought to the text of Scripture intentionally. They are rules that can be held to in order to properly handle the Word of truth.

Scripture Interprets Scripture

The Bible is not a collection of disconnected truths. It is a unified whole, revealing a single author (God) across many human writers. Because of that, every part of Scripture must be read in light of the whole. Paul does not contradict James. Jesus does not correct Moses. Prophets do not override apostles. Every word must be interpreted in the context of every other word. When you do not understand a passage, look elsewhere in Scripture for clarity. The unclear is made clear by the plain, not the other way around.

This is why isolated interpretation is so dangerous. You cannot extract a verse from its context, assert a meaning, and call it truth. You must trace the thread of God's meaning from book to book and from testament to testament. When Scripture interprets Scripture, you arrive at

---

7. "The Chicago Statement on Biblical Inerrancy," *Evangelical Review of Theology*, 4, no.1 (1980).

something that is unbreakable. You arrive at truth.

To illustrate what I am driving at, Romans 3:10–11 provides the perfect case study. It says,

> None is righteous, no, not one;
> no one understands;
> no one seeks for God.

Seems pretty cut and dry right? Not so fast. Two things need to be considered here. First, Paul is quoting a Psalm in this verse. We need to know whether he is using it in context or if he is using it to support a different point. Second, is this obvious reading (that *no one* is righteous, and *no one* seeks God) supported by the rest of Scripture? Unfortunately, this isn't as cut and dry as many make it out to be. There are two main counters to note here. First, Paul is quoting the Psalms. Specifically, he is pulling from Psalm 14. The problem is that this Psalm directly says that some are righteous. It says, "For God is with the generation of the righteous" (Psalm 14:5). Second, Scripture *regularly* calls people righteous. One quick example is about Noah. Genesis 6:9 says, "Noah was a righteous man." Scripture also says similar things about those who understand and seek after God. If all of this is true, then the normal reading of Romans 3:10–11 does not say what it seems to be saying. If it did, then we have a logical contradiction and can rightly reject Scripture as being fallible and errant. That is not necessary, however, because there is a valid explanation that upholds both "none is righteous, no, not one" and there are those who are "righteous." Paul's point is that there isn't a human being who can rightly say that they didn't fall. He is *not* saying that no one is righteous or can't be righteous. One sin, no matter how small, is enough to disqualify someone from being in the presence of God. That is Paul's point. Every human *except Jesus* has failed to attain the standard necessary to be in God's presence without intervention. It is only through Jesus, via faith, that one can be saved.

Logical Consistency Matters

Truth cannot contradict itself. That is as basic as it is forgotten. Many Christians are willing to hold beliefs that, when placed side by side, tear each other apart. This is confusion, not faith. We must be willing to examine every belief in light of the whole and ask, "Can these things stand together without collapsing?"

If two interpretations of Scripture create logical tension, then one of them—or both—is wrong. There is no third option. Logic does not supersede Scripture, but it does help us detect faulty interpretation. If your reading of one verse creates contradiction with another, then you have misread. The problem is not the Bible. It is you, or whoever is doing the interpreting. We all have a tendency to either ignore or downplay passages that don't fit neatly into our theological systems. The difficulty with doing this is that it directly pits Scripture against Scripture, which we have already established is no good. Scripture *interprets*

Scripture. Thus, when one passage seems to contradict an-other, our job as interpreters is to see how the two ideas fit together without the contradiction. This takes both a very solid understanding of how we are to go about interpreting Scripture and a mind that has been trained to look for coherence (logical consistency).

There are cases where what seems to be plainly said is not the correct answer but, if we use logic, we can "fix" the interpretive problem. To see how logic serves faithful interpretation, let's examine a commonly misunderstood passage where a surface-level reading produces confusion.

A plain reading of Luke 22:19–20, without applying logic to it, says that the bread and wine are literally Jesus' body and blood. The passage is as follows:

> And he took bread, and when he had giv-en thanks, he broke it and gave it to them, saying, "This is my body, which is given for you. Do this in remembrance of me." And likewise the cup after they had eaten, saying, "This cup that is poured out for you is the new covenant in my blood."

Reading this "plainly" suggests that it is Christ's lit-eral body and blood. However, logically, this doesn't stand. Jesus is standing *right there*. Unless one wants to posit that his body and blood were in two places at once, and there is no reason to do so, this passage is pointing toward a symbol. The bread is *symbolically* his body and the wine is his blood. Anyone who was with him during that meal would have intuitively understood it that way. It is only as we try to read this passage after the fact that it seems to become unclear. But with a modest application of logic, the meaning becomes clear.

It's not enough to affirm symbolism because Protestant tradition says so. The passage itself demands it. Luke doesn't signal a shift into poetry or metaphor; he records a historical event. If Jesus hands his disciples bread and says, 'This is my body,' while still seated in his own body, the context itself disqualifies literalism. Unless his body is simultaneously on the table and in the seat, and there's no textual reason to believe that, then
Jesus was not being literal. The truth is simpler: Jesus used the bread and wine as symbols. The logic is not a threat to Scripture. Instead, it's a necessary ally in discerning what Scripture actually means.

No Verse Cancels Another

This point cannot be overstated. Every verse in Scripture is true given the proper biblical, literary, and historical context and authorial intent.[8] No verse nullifies another. You

---

8. Part of hermeneutics is understanding the literary genre. A historical account, for example, can include someone saying something false. In this case, the historical account is being truthfully laid out. Someone lied or was wrong. When this happens, Scripture is faithfully recording the scenario, but one must not assume that we are then to do whatever the person did or said. That would be improperly interpreting the text.

cannot use John 10:28 to erase Hebrews 6. You cannot wield Ephesians 2:8–9 against James 2:24. The temptation to elevate some verses and minimize others is subtle. But it is always a hermeneutical failure.

Inerrancy demands consistency. Every text must be brought into agreement with every other text, not by forcing them to conform to your theology, but by letting them interpret each other in full, honest context. If your reading of one verse forces you to explain away another, start over. Your interpretation is wrong. I have had to change positions on quite a few doctrines because of this. When I hit a verse and I think to myself, "That can't be saying what it seems to be saying," odds are pretty good that I have let my personal theology interfere with the passage's meaning, unless my concern arises from other passages of Scripture. In which case, it is necessary to figure out how the verses work together rather than choosing one verse over another.

Avoid Emotional and Traditional Bias

Your background does not define truth. Neither do your feelings. Many interpretations are held not because they are true, but because they are familiar. People grow up hearing a verse taught one way and never question it. Others come to Scripture with emotional investments that cloud their judgment.

You must ruthlessly set those things aside.

It doesn't matter what your denomination taught, what your pastor believes, or what feels right. You are not allowed to edit Scripture with your feelings or guard your theology with tradition. Let the text speak. Let it destroy your categories if necessary. Only then will you understand it. The above discussion on presuppositions fits in this category. We must not let preconceived ideas dictate what the text *must* say. Instead, we need to learn to let the text speak for itself. We are to conform to Scripture, not make Scripture conform to us.[9]

Truth Requires Discipline and Humility

This is not for the lazy. Truth requires work, a *lot* of work. You must slow down. You must ask hard questions. You must read the whole Bible and refuse to interpret any verse in isolation. You must demand that every belief aligns with every other truth in Scripture. There is nothing easy about this. To do what is laid out in this chapter is to accept the hard life of truly delving into Scripture, not to prove your position, but to truly seek what God is saying. This leads directly into the need for humility.

In addition to lots of work, truth requires humility. You must be willing to be wrong. You must be willing to change your mind. You must allow Scripture to correct you, even if it costs you dearly. And it will. It may cost you theological systems, denominational affiliations, or cherished teachings. But if you truly want the one truth, you

---

9. Bernard Ramm, *Protestant Biblical Interpretation: A Textbook of Hermeneutics* (Grand Rapids: Baker, 1970), 115-16.

must lay those down. I have been writing an entire book because I was wrong on a position. I was telling Scripture that X must be true even though Scripture disagreed with me. I taught that position publicly, via a different book, and now I need to repent of that in the same way. We cannot go to Scripture and assume we are correct. Let Scripture guide you, through the Holy Spirit, into all truth.

There is no shortcut to truth. But there is a path. Strive to read the Bible with consistency, with logic, without bias, and with a deep hunger, leaning on the Holy Spirit to be conformed to what is true. That is what God expects. That is what Scripture demands, and it is the only way to rightly interpret the Word of God.

What About Mystery?

Christians, both lay and scholarly, tend to have a willingness to appeal to mystery if they don't know the answer to something. For example, how the Trinity can work is often explained to an extent, but most Christians will end up appealing to mystery at one point or another. The problem is that biblical mystery is not the same as ours is today. When an English-speaking person says that something is a mystery, it is rarely in the biblical sense. It is often more in the sense that we *can't* understand something even though we "know" it. G. K. Beale and Benjamin Gladd define biblical mystery this way:

We will define *mystery* generally as *the rev-*

> *elation of God's partially hidden wisdom,*
> *particularly as it concerns events occurring in*
> *the "latter days."* As we will see, scholars are
> on the right track when they define *mystery*
> as *divine wisdom that was previously "hid-*
> *den" but has now been "revealed."*[10]

They go on to note that biblical mystery *does* have similar connotations to contemporary uses of the term by saying that it contains the idea of "knowledge that is somewhat baffling."[11] From a truth perspective, what they are saying functionally is that mystery is that which has either not been fully revealed, or that which has been revealed but is not easy to understand. I do not disagree with this. What I do disagree with is the idea that we can be happy with contradictions in our interpretations of Scripture or our use of reason by appealing to "mystery". At no point does the Bible support the idea that mystery allows for actual contradictions.

To go back to the Trinity example, the Trinity is upheld as fact while, at the same time, it is argued that we cannot understand it. Divine mystery is appealed to in order to make this work. This *might* be true. If the Trinity, as revealed in Scripture and logically deduced, is truly beyond the comprehension of humans (due to humans lacking

---

10. G. K, Beale and Benjamin L Gladd, *Hidden but Now Revealed: A Biblical Theology of Mystery* (Downers Grove, IL: IVP Academic, 2014), 16.

11. Ibid.

the necessary logical abilities or the truth not being fully revealed), then yes, this could be true. But the challenge is that the Trinity as it is traditionally upheld comes with logical *contradictions*. To say that the Father is fully God (i.e., he possesses everything that God is and has), the Son is fully God, and the Spirit is fully God, but that the Father is *not* the Son and the Son is *not* the Spirit is fundamentally contradictory. Mystery cannot be appealed to in this case. If we appeal to mystery because we are upholding two or more truly contradictory statements, then something needs to change. For more than a few, the solution to this problem has been to reject the Trinity as unbiblical or philosophically incoherent. However, the solution is not to throw the baby out with the bathwater. Instead, we should be looking for a new way to take the biblical data (which clearly shows some form of a Trinity) and rework the metaphysics (the theory that accounts for the factual (biblical) data, logical consistency, and explanatory power of the Trinity).[12] In the case of the Trinity, the Bible holds the factual data. It is God revealing himself to us and we see this in the form of the Father, Son, and Holy Spirit. The Trinity, as it has been traditionally upheld, is an attempt to logically explain

---

12. William Hasker, *Metaphysics: Constructing a World View* (Downers Grove, IL: IVP Academic, 1983), 26. Hasker argues that any metaphysical theory needs to account for these three things, which is true. Anytime we take the factual data for something, see how the data fits logically, and demonstrate how it explains the data, we are doing metaphysics. Throughout this book, I have appealed to Scripture as the ultimate source of truth that God has given us access to. This is because I have crafted a metaphysic on the Word of God.

the biblical data. That said, if it is logically inconsistent, or if it does not properly account for the factual data, then the metaphysic must be reworked. Doing this work is not changing God. Rather, it is trying to accurately portray and explain what he has revealed about himself. My work on Structural Theism is exactly this attempt. Take the biblical data and construct a metaphysic that can handle it. Doing the opposite is an example of authority confusion.

To reiterate, mystery can be appealed to only in cases where the data is insufficient to make a robust claim, or when something is truly beyond comprehension. It cannot be used to uphold contradictions.

The Role of the Holy Spirit

The primary focus of this book is on how you as an individual can find the truth in Scripture and in life; however, we must not forget that the Holy Spirit plays an integral role in understanding God and his Word. It is not presently my intent to provide a full defense for the Spirit's role, but I cannot, in good conscience, proceed without addressing him briefly. John 14:26 explicitly states that the Spirit is a "helper," or rather *the* "helper," who will lead us into all truth (John 16:13). It is through him that we can truly understand who God is. Additionally, Scripture states that the wisdom of this world is foolishness to God (1 Corinthians 3:19). If that is true, and God's ways are "higher" than man's (Isaiah 55:8–9), then it is logically true to say that we need God to show us the right path. This happens when we lean on the Spirit, utilize God's Word, and apply our minds to understanding and obeying what we find.

Summary

This chapter argues that every passage in Scripture has only one correct interpretation, even if that interpretation has multiple layers or referents. The example of Hosea 11:1 is used to show that God can intend more than one legitimate referent (Israel and Christ) within the same true interpretation. Applications of Scripture, while numerous, must flow from the correct interpretation rather than distort or ignore context. Sound hermeneutics demands that Scripture interpret Scripture, that interpretations maintain logical consistency, that no verse be used to nullify another, and that emotional or traditional biases be set aside. Truth requires discipline, humility, and willingness to be corrected by Scripture. Mystery, in the biblical sense, refers to truth that was once hidden but is now revealed (though perhaps still difficult to understand) and should never be used to excuse logical contradictions. The Holy Spirit plays an essential role in guiding believers into truth, working alongside disciplined study and contextual reading.

Discussion Questions:

Summarize this chapter in your own words.

How does affirming that one passage can have multiple legitimate referents within one interpretation change your approach to passages often considered "only about" one thing?

What dangers arise when we treat personal application as interchangeable with interpretation, and how might that affect doctrinal accuracy?

When two passages seem to contradict, what steps should you take to bring them into harmony without forcing them into your theological system?

How can you recognize and intentionally set aside emotional or traditional biases when approaching a text?

In what situations is it legitimate to appeal to "mystery," and how can you avoid using it to cover up contradictions in your theology?

What practical steps can you take to rely on the Holy Spirit's guidance in your interpretation while still exercising disciplined study?

CHAPTER SEVEN

WHY TRUTH DEMANDS ACTION

HOPEFULLY, YOU HAVE SEEN by now that truth exists, and that for every question, every doctrine, and every moral issue, there is a single truth statement that actually reflects reality. Truth is not a matter of personal perception, cultural consensus, or emotional resonance. It is objective, singular, and unyielding. And because it is objective, it is knowable. Not always easily, instantly, or fully in this life. However, that which God wants us to know, or that we need to know, has been revealed. Like any good investigator, the believer is called to dig, sift, and test, following the evidence, the logic, and above all, the Word of God, to discover what is true. This skill of truth discernment is a necessity, especially when it comes to the things of God.

If we don't know what truth is (or worse, if we think objective, universal truth changes depending on the person or the situation), we will not just lose arguments. We will lose our footing, and let Satan gain a foothold (Ephesians 4:27). A believer who is not grounded in truth is like a soldier going to war without a weapon, without armor, and without training. When we enter the cultural battlefield, whether we're witnessing to others, defending our faith, or just trying to stand firm, we will falter unless we are rooted in what is true. Above all else, Scripture is where we must root ourselves deeply.[1]

And being rooted in the truth involves acting on it. You can have the right theology, the right apologetics, and the right answers, but if you do not live in obedience to the truth, your knowledge is hollow. Jesus calls us to submit to the truth, not simply to admire it. Truth, by its very nature, demands a response. It makes a claim on your life. It exposes what is false, including the lies we like to tell ourselves. It does not care about your preferences, your upbringing, your denomination, or your comfort. It asks only one thing: will you conform your life to it?

This is the real dividing line. It is not whether someone claims to believe in Jesus or even believes in truth in a general sense. The question is whether they are willing to submit to what is true *when it costs them*. When it exposes a wrong belief. When it challenges their tradition. When it convicts them of sin. At that point, people tend to do one of two things: either they align their life and theology to the truth, or they twist the truth to fit their life and theology. The former is obedience. The latter is idolatry, and a more dangerous road has rarely been travelled.

The point of this chapter is not merely to reiterate

---

1. See Psalm 1 for a quick, yet powerful engagement with this idea.

that truth matters. You already know that. The point is to say this: if truth is singular, knowable, and binding (even if complex and contextual), then it is not enough to passively acknowledge it. You must act on it. You must believe what is true. Live what is true. Teach what is true, and reject what is false, no matter how tempting or popular it may be. There is no neutral ground. There is no safe middle between truth and error. Every day you are either conforming your mind to the truth of God or conforming the truth of God to your mind. To put it in a different way, you are either moving toward God, or you are backsliding away from God. Stagnancy in faith, though a popular way of describing one's faith, does not really exist. It is like learning a language. Unless you are dedicated to that language day in and day out, you will not continue progressing enough to become fluent and, if you don't use it, you lose it. You don't just stagnate. You actively move the wrong direction.

This is why we have laid such a strong foundation up to this point. Because without a firm understanding of what truth is—how it works, why it matters, and what it requires—we cannot move forward in the Christian life with any confidence. In both past and future books, I apply this framework to some of the most important questions a person can ask: Who is God? What is salvation? Can we trust Scripture? These are the truths upon which eternity hangs. And if you are not grounded in the nature of truth itself, you will be tossed around by every wind of doctrine (Ephesians 4:14).

So let me ask plainly: Are you prepared to let the truth

reshape your assumptions, your doctrine, your morality, and your life? Or will you cling to what is familiar, comforting, or culturally approved, even if it means compromising the truth?

If you want to follow Christ faithfully, you need to submit to the truth. You need to act on it. Because truth—real, objective, singular truth—demands nothing less.

Looking to the Future: What Happens When We Divide God's Word?

In this book, I've argued that truth is always singular, even if our understanding of it is limited. Every question has one right answer since reality does not contradict itself, and neither does Scripture. But this naturally leads to a deeper and more unsettling question: If truth is singular, then why do so many Christians treat some truths as optional?

The modern church has inherited a set of categories ("essential," "nonessential," "primary," "secondary," etc.) that are often used to justify doctrinal disagreement. These terms are meant to promote peace and unity, but in practice, they've created a theological minimalism that undermines the very thing we claim to protect: the truth.

Imagine a legal system that said only murder mattered, and every other law was "nonessential." Or a marriage where one partner said only fidelity counted, but love, respect, and faithfulness in small things were secondary. What kind of foundation would that build?

In the same way, when we divide the Word of God into essential and nonessential truths, we compromise the coherence of God's revelation and open the door to relativism within the church.

In the books that follow this one, I explore where this categorization came from, why it persists, and why it must be abandoned. Other derivative works will include a robust philosophical defense of Contextual Absolutism and a full hermeneutics model. If you found this book helpful, those next works will give you the historical and theological tools to resist doctrinal minimalism and reclaim the fullness of biblical truth.

Additionally, this book has laid the groundwork, the foundation, for my method in other works. Any book I write will have Contextual Absolutism as its base. It explains why I am willing to go against tradition and why I interpret passages the way I do. That said, it is only the foundation, a teaser if you will, to the full development of Contextual Absolutism.

Ultimately, what has been presented in this work requires at least three more books to fully flesh out. It needs a book that lays out the hermeneutics in explicit form, a philosophy book that robustly lays out the formal logic of Contextual Absolutism, and a book that directly engages the challenge of dividing God's Word into "primary," "secondary," and "tertiary" categories. If this book has intrigued you (or been found wanting due to its short, lay-accessible, and polemical style), then be on the lookout for those future works. They probably won't be any less polemical, but they will engage much more with the literature.

Summary

This chapter argues that truth is objective, singular, and knowable, and that Christians must submit to it and live by it. Truth is not shaped by personal preference, culture, or emotion, and to be grounded in it is essential for spiritual stability and effective witness. Intellectual assent alone is insufficient; obedience is the true test of whether one has embraced the truth. The author warns against dividing God's Word into "essential" and "nonessential" categories, contending that such distinctions lead to theological minimalism and compromise. The chapter closes by pointing to future works that will further develop the philosophical, hermeneutical, and theological framework of Contextual Absolutism, challenging believers to conform their lives and doctrines wholly to the truth of God.

Discussion Questions:

Summarize this chapter in your own words.

What are some practical ways you can move beyond knowing truth intellectually to living it out daily in obedience?

When faced with a truth that challenges your tradition or personal comfort, how do you typically respond, and what would it look like to submit to it instead?

How might the church's use of "essential" and "nonessential" categories impact unity, doctrine, and discipleship, both positively and negatively?

What dangers arise when Christians passively acknowledge truth without acting on it, and how can you guard against this tendency in your own life?

In what ways does rooting yourself in Scripture help you withstand cultural pressures and false teaching?

How could adopting the perspective of Contextual Absolutism shape the way you approach theological disagreement and interpret Scripture?

CHAPTER EIGHT

FORMALIZING CONTEXTUAL ABSOLUTISM

I F THE AIM OF this book has been to demonstrate that truth is singular, knowable, and essential for theology, then this chapter exists to formally name and define the model that makes that possible: Contextual Absolutism.

Contextual Absolutism is a philosophical viewpoint and a methodological commitment. It insists that all true statements correspond to reality as it is, but that each claim must be interpreted and assessed in light of its contextual parameters. Without this, contradiction masquerades as mystery, tradition stifles revision, and doctrine drifts into incoherence.

Formal Definition

Contextual Absolutism is the epistemological model that holds the following:

For every meaningful proposition, there exists one and only one truth statement that corresponds to reality. That truth statement includes contextual qualifiers that determine its scope, application, or subjective referent, but the truth itself remains singular, exclusive, and, in most cases, discoverable.

Put differently: *truth is absolute*, but to *state* it rightly requires the articulation of its *context* unless the context is successfully implied. Any apparent contradiction between two truth claims is either the result of misframed contexts, poor articulation, or theological error, not mystery.

Core Axioms

1. Singularity of Truth

There is only one truth for any given question or proposition. This applies equally to metaphysics, ethics, theology, science, and preference. Competing truth claims cannot both be true in the same context.

2. Contextual Framing

All statements must be understood *within a specific context* in order to retain their truth. "God is love" is true, but it must be understood properly (i.e., the correct God and the correct idea of love must be in mind). Provided that the proper context is given for the above statement, it is universally true. However, some statements are true, but only when referring to a specific person or place. For example, "pineapple on pizza is gross" is false universally but true *to me.* The context ("to me") makes the statement coherent, not relativistic.

3. Discoverability and Revision

Truth may be difficult to discern, but it is not beyond reach. Over time, better exegesis, better definitions, and better metaphysical models lead to the refinement of truth claims. This requires humility and the willingness to revise doctrine in light of new insights. Mystery is still maintained as a viable solution but *only* in situations where God has not revealed the whole truth. It cannot be appealed to if one is trying to hold two contradictory statements.

4. Ontological Stability and Epistemic Contingency

Unless the referent itself is unstable,[1] truth does not change, but our perception or articulation of it might. God's nature is not altered when our theology about him improves. Our epistemology changes; God's ontology does not.

5. God as the One Absolute

God is the only non-contingent source of truth. Everything else is derived and dependent. Therefore, truth begins and ends in God, not in philosophy, not in consensus, and certainly not in tradition.

---

1. See the illustrations below.

Illustrations in Practice

Pineapple on Pizza

The claim "pineapple is gross on pizza" is either false or incomplete unless framed properly: "To me, pineapple is gross on pizza." This is a subjective preference, but the *truth* of that statement is still *singular* and based on a real referent—*my preference*. This referent is inherently unstable. If I change my preference later, the new truth is also singular and contextual.

Doctrinal Revisions

Consider the doctrine of divine immutability. Classical models may claim, "God cannot change in any way." But Scripture affirms that God regrets, responds, and is emotionally affected. The classical claim and the biblical witness cannot both be true in the same context. Contextual Absolutism forces us to clarify our terms, define change, and rebuild doctrine with coherence when necessary, rather than hide behind mystery.

Moral Relativism?

A relativist might say, "Everyone has their own truth." But Contextual Absolutism would respond: "Everyone can have a different *contextual truth claim*, but those claims are still either accurate or inaccurate depending on the real referent." Truth remains exclusive; subjectivity just shifts the reference point, not the absoluteness of the truth.

Theological Implications

1. Mystery Cannot Be Contradiction

Doctrinal tension must never be resolved by asserting two mutually exclusive claims as simultaneously true. Theological integrity demands precision. Mystery can mean hidden knowledge, or even "baffling" knowledge,[2] but it cannot be contradiction in disguise.

2. Doctrine is Subject to Correction

Because truth is singular, we must continually refine doctrines to reflect it. Historical confessions, while useful, are not authoritative if they misstate or misframe the truth. This is the method behind *Structural Theism*, *Structural Kenotic Christology*, and every model I propose elsewhere.

3. Unity Requires Clarity

The church cannot unify around contradiction or ambiguity. If we cannot agree on what God is like, how salvation works, or how truth operates, we cannot walk together in truth. Contextual Absolutism seeks clarity—not division—for the sake of fidelity.

The Formal Logic of Contextual Absolutism

To define truth with rigor, we must outline the internal logic of this model.

Basic Form

Every truth claim under Contextual Absolutism

---

2. Beale, *Hidden but Now Revealed*, 16.

should be expressible in the form:

[Subject] + [Predicate] + [Context] = True

In contrast to traditional correspondence theories, Contextual Absolutism demonstrates that truth *requires* context in every case. This context can be implied, but it must still be there.

Examples:

- "God is omnipotent." Ontologically true, but it is not communicated as true to someone who defines omnipotence as "being able to make a rock too heavy to lift." In other words, it still requires context, even if that context is implied.

- "God regretted making man." True *in the narrative context of Genesis 6*.

- "God is real." True, if one is talking about the *correct* God.

- "Pineapple on pizza is disgusting to me." True *within my current taste context*. If I were in a conversation, the context could be implied. For example, I could say, "Pineapple on pizza is disgusting." It is implied that it is disgusting *to me* even though I did not explicitly say so.

Conditional Form

Conditional truths appear in Scripture and experience:

If X, then Y (provided Z)

Z functions as a condition and is part of the context outlined above but is not the whole of the context. Beyond standard context, a truth claim can have specific conditions in order for it to be true. The main difference is that this condition must happen before a truth claim goes into effect. The basic form above merely demonstrates that context is needed. In the conditional form, the same context is applied, but a condition is also required.

Examples:

- "If you repent, you will be forgiven." True *under the gospel*, but not necessarily true when repenting to humans.

- "If you will indeed obey my voice and keep my covenant, you shall be my treasured possession among all peoples" (Exodus 19:5). True but the condition *if you will indeed obey my voice and keep my covenant* is required for the truth claim to "trigger," and this has a specific context beyond the condition. It is a promise from *Yahweh to Israel*.

Such claims are valid truth statements under limited

condition sets, which are real but not eternal. Contextual Absolutism affirms conditional truths as legitimate truth expressions with delimited scope.

Conflict Resolution Logic

When two apparent truths conflict:

1. **Identify Contexts**: Are they speaking in the same frame?

2. **Clarify Definitions**: Are they using words consistently?

3. **Test against Reality and Revelation**: Which one corresponds?

4. **Discard the False**: Two contradictory statements cannot both be true.

"Jesus is God."
"Jesus is not God."
Cannot both be true under the same context. One is false. Period.

This non-relativistic clarity is what Contextual Absolutism demands of all theology. If given the same context, these cannot both be true. *But* both statements can be true if given different contexts. "Jesus is God" is true if the context is just on whether he is divine. "Jesus is not God" is true if the context is based around the Trinity. *Alone*, he is not the whole of God. So, one can rightly say Jesus is *not*

God *if*, by that, they mean that God must consist of Father, Son, and Holy Spirit. Acknowledging this does not diminish Christ's divinity in anyway, it simply acknowledges that context can change whether a statement is true or not. When applied to studying Scripture, understanding what Scripture is actually saying, based on context, can solve a huge number of apparent contradictions.

Conclusion

Contextual Absolutism is the view that every truth claim must be evaluated as a singular, absolute proposition framed within its necessary context, whether ontological, semantic, conditional, or subjective. Additionally, it is the epistemological engine behind my entire theological model. It is the reason I can reject traditions, rebuild doctrines, and assert theological clarity without apology. It is the lens through which I evaluate every claim be it biblical, theological, metaphysical, or personal.

This model defines truth and it demands action. If what we believe does not correspond to the real, revealed, coherent truth of God, then it must be revised. If doctrine contradicts itself, it must be rewritten. If tradition distorts Scripture, it must be discarded.

Because there is only one truth, and it is worth fighting for.

A Brief Call to Action

If you found value in this book, please consider leaving an honest review on your favorite book review site (Amazon, BookBub, Goodreads, etc.). Reviews are tremendously helpful to authors. They are, in many ways, the lifeblood of a book and I highly appreciate each one that I receive.

Also, if you are interested in receiving updates on books, book reviews, and other short teachings that I publish, you can follow me on:

- Facebook (Meta): L. J. Anderson at www.facebook.com/profile.php?id=61553506423559

- YouTube: L. J. Anderson at www.youtube.com/@ljandersonbooks

- My website: www.ljandersonbooks.com

ALSO BY L. J. ANDERSON

Books

- *Contending for the Truth: A Biblical Look at Thirteen Contentious Doctrines*

- *Salvation by Faith Alone? Living in the Nuance of Faith and Works* (coming soon!)

Short Academic Books

- *Theology and Apologetics: An Examination of How and Where They Intersect*

- *The Moral Argument: Is It Worth Having in Your Apologetic Repertoire?*

- *The Inerrancy of Scripture: An Overview and Defense*

- *Tribulation as Wrath: Rethinking the Timing of God's Judgment*

- *Legalism: The Ethical System That Becomes a False God*

- *Hebrews 6:1–8: An Exegetical Strike Against Eternal Security* (coming soon!)

- *Gnosticism: A Biblical and Historical Response* (coming soon!)

BIBLIOGRAPHY

Allison, Gregg R. *The Baker Compact Dictionary of Theological Terms.* Grand Rapids, MI: Baker Books, 2016.

Anderson, L. J. *Contending for the Truth: A Biblical Look at Thirteen Contentious Doctrines.* Billings, MT: Lamad Press, 2025.

Anderson, L. J. *The Inerrancy of Scripture: An Overview and Defense.* Billings, MT: Lamad Press, 2025.

Anderson, L. J. *Tribulation as Wrath: Rethinking the Timing of God's Judgment.* Billings, MT: Lamad Press, 2025.

Andrew, Stephen L. "Biblical Inerrancy," *Chafer Theological Seminary Journal* 8.1 (Winter 2002).

Beale, G. K, and Benjamin L Gladd. *Hidden but Now Revealed: A Biblical Theology of Mystery.* Downers Grove, IL: IVP Academic, 2014.

Berding, Kenneth, and Jonathan Lunde, eds. *Three Views on the New Testament Use of the Old Testament*. Grand Rapids: Zondervan, 2007.

Bird, Michael F., and Scott Harrower, eds. *Trinity without Hierarchy: Reclaiming Nicene Orthodoxy in Evangelical Theology.* Grand Rapids, MI: Kregel Academic, 2019.

Campbell, Ronnie P., and Christopher Gnanakan, eds. *Do Christians, Muslims, and Jews Worship the Same God? Four Views*. Grand Rapids, MI: Zondervan Academic, 2019.

Diamond, Lisa M., and Molly Butterworth, "Questioning Gender and Sexual Identity: Dynamic Links over Time," *Sex Roles*, 59 (5–6): 365–376. doi:10.1007/s11199-008-9425-3.

Dockery, David S., and Christopher W. Morgan, eds. *Christian Higher Education: Faith, Teaching, and Learning in the Evangelical Tradition*. Wheaton, IL: Crossway, 2018.

France, R. T. *Matthew: An Introduction and* Commentary. Downers Grove, IL: InterVarsity Press, 1985.

Geisler, Norman. *The Big Book of Christian Apologetics: An A to Z Guide*. Grand Rapids, MI: Baker Books, 2012.

Gould, Paul, Travis Dickinson, and Keith Loftin, *Stand Firm: Apologetics and the Brilliance of the Gospel*. Nashville, TN: B&H Academic, 2018.

Grudem, Wayne. *Systematic Theology: An Introduction to Biblical Doctrine*. Grand Rapids, MI: Zondervan Academic, 2020.

Hasker, William. *Metaphysics: Constructing a World View*. Downers Grove, IL: IVP Academic, 1983.

Jastrow, Robert. *God and the Astronomers*. New York: W. W. Norton & Company, 1992.

Mcleod, Saul. "Humanistic Approach in Psychology (Humanism): Definition & Examples." *Simply Psychology*. December 20, 2023. https://www.simplypsychology.org/humanistic.html.

Olson, Roger E. *Arminian Theology: Myths and Realities*. Downers Grove, IL: InterVarsity Press, 2006.

Peckham, John C. *The Love of God: A Canonical Model*. Downers Grove, IL: InterVarsity Press, 2015.

Ramm, Bernard. *Protestant Biblical Interpretation: A Textbook of Hermeneutics*. Grand Rapids: Baker, 1970.

Runzo, Joseph. "God, Commitment, and Other Faiths: Pluralism vs. Relativism." *Faith and Philosophy*, 5 (1988): 343–364.

"The Chicago Statement on Biblical Inerrancy," *Evangelical Review of Theology*, 4, no.1 (1980).

Thomas, Robert L. "Biblical Hermeneutics: Single Meaning and Its Effects." Paper presented at the Chafer Conference. *The Master's Seminary*, 2009. https://www.deanbible.org/dbmfiles/notes/2 009-ChaferConf-Thomas-Paper-02.pdf.

Vanhoozer, Kevin J. *Mere Christian Hermeneutics: Transfiguring What It Means to Read the Bible Theologically*. Grand Rapids, MI: Zondervan Academic, 2024.

A NOTE TO SCHOLARS AND CRITICS

This book was not peer-reviewed in the tradition-al, blind-review sense. It was published independently through Lamad Press as part of a broader effort to make rigorous, biblically grounded theology more accessible and transparent. That choice was intentional and reflects a dif-ferent but equally serious approach to scholarly engage-ment.

Whereas traditional peer review filters access to the academic conversation, open review invites that conversa-tion to happen in full view of others. Rather than submit-ting this work to a handful of anonymous reviewers behind closed doors, I have released it publicly for anyone—scholar or layperson—to read, test, and critique. I believe truth is not threatened by transparency. It thrives on it.

This model is not about bypassing scrutiny. It's about placing the burden of proof where it belongs: on the quality of the argument, the clarity of the logic, and the faithfulness to Scripture. If this work is flawed, let that be shown in the open. And if it is sound, then let it be recognized—not because it passed through a gatekeeper, but because it stood up under real engagement.

To that end:

- Many of my full manuscripts are available for free on Academia.edu.

- I am more than willing to provide free copies of my books to scholars who are open to giving them a fair reading.

- I welcome pushback, critique, and dialogue. I do not write for validation. I write for the sake of theological clarity, biblical fidelity, and the health of the church.

Thank you for reading. If this work raises questions, I hope you'll pursue them. And if it invites disagreement, I hope you'll engage, not to dismiss, but to sharpen. That is how theology moves forward, and that is the kind of scholarship I aim to practice.

L. J. Anderson

About the Author

L. J. Anderson is an independent scholar, author, and founder of **Lamad Press**, an academic imprint dedicated to publishing biblically grounded theological works. He holds a Master of Divinity and is currently pursuing a PhD in theology, where his dissertation research focuses on developing a new model of God. This model seeks to offer a coherent and biblically faithful framework capable of addressing longstanding challenges to the doctrine of God—particularly those related to the Trinity.

This work represents a piece of that broader research agenda, contributing to the reevaluation of traditional theological formulations in light of Scripture. Anderson aims to bridge the gap between philosophical coherence and scriptural fidelity, crafting theological models that remain both rigorous and accessible.

He has published several books through Lamad Press, including *The Inerrancy of Scripture* and *The Moral Argument*, and his writings are indexed in Google Scholar. As a disabled veteran, he is able to devote his time to research, writing, and publishing, with the long-term goal of establishing Lamad Press as a trusted source for independent academic theology.

He is also the founder of **Lamad Christian Books**, a curated online bookstore offering academic and devotional Christian works, Christian fiction, and clean non-Christian fiction. You can learn more at **ljandersonbooks.com** and **lamadpress.com**.